Minority Ethnic Voices in Healthcare Professions

of related interest

Occupational Therapy, Disability Activism, and Me
Challenging Ableism in Healthcare
Georgia Vine
ISBN 978 1 83997 667 4
eISBN 978 1 83997 668 1

Antiracist Occupational Therapy
Unsettling the Status Quo
Edited by Musharrat J. Ahmed-Landeryou
Foreword by Professor Elelwani Ramugondo
ISBN 978 1 83997 574 5
eISBN 978 1 83997 575 2

Occupational Therapy Disruptors
What Global OT Practice Can Teach Us About Innovation, Culture, and Community
Sheela Roy Ivlev
Foreword by Juman Simaan
ISBN 978 1 83997 665 0
eISBN 978 1 83997 666 7

Minority Ethnic Voices in Healthcare Professions

Strategies for Career Empowerment and Creating Inclusive Settings

HEENA MAHMOOD

Jessica Kingsley Publishers
London and Philadelphia

First published in Great Britain in 2025 by Jessica Kingsley Publishers
An imprint of John Murray Press

1

Copyright © Heena Mahmood 2025

The right of Heena Mahmood to be identified as the Author of the Work has been asserted by her in accordance with the Copyright, Designs and Patents Act 1988.

All rights reserved. No part of this publication may be reproduced, stored in a retrieval system, or transmitted, in any form or by any means without the prior written permission of the publisher, nor be otherwise circulated in any form of binding or cover other than that in which it is published and without a similar condition being imposed on the subsequent purchaser.

A CIP catalogue record for this title is available from the
British Library and the Library of Congress

ISBN 978 1 80501 154 5

eISBN 978 1 80501 155 2

Printed and bound in Great Britain by CPI Group (UK) Ltd

Jessica Kingsley Publishers' policy is to use papers that are natural, renewable and recyclable products and made from wood grown in sustainable forests. The logging and manufacturing processes are expected to conform to the environmental regulations of the country of origin.

Jessica Kingsley Publishers
Carmelite House
50 Victoria Embankment
London EC4Y 0DZ

www.jkp.com

John Murray Press
Part of Hodder & Stoughton Ltd
An Hachette Company

The authorised representative in the EEA is Hachette Ireland,
8 Castlecourt Centre, Dublin 15, D15 XTP3, Ireland.

Contents

Preface. 7

1. Introduction. 11
2. Racial Inequalities 21
3. Case Study 1: Allied Health Professions 36
4. Case Study 2: A Nurse's Journey 57
5. Case Study 3: From Chaplain to EDI Lead 69
6. Case Study 4: The Chief Executive Officer 84
7. Case Study 5: Clinical Support Worker (Band 3) 101
8. Allyship and Its Importance. 112
9. Allyship Case Study 1: Being a Mentor. 121
10. Allyship Case Study 2: An Ally's Experience 134
11. Allyship Case Study 3: Accomplished Ally 145
12. Final Thoughts 165

Acronyms. 175

Acknowledgements. 176

References. 179

Preface

When I first started working in the NHS, I remember how awkward I felt being the only Asian person in my team, not to mention the only one wearing a hijab. Growing up surrounded by people who were black, white and Asian in school and college and then going to a place where I was the odd one out felt very strange.

One day, I went to see a patient with my supervisee to provide a teaching session on how to complete a physiotherapy assessment. During the assessment, the patient made a racist remark, and my colleague's response (as a white male) was to turn bright red. I challenged the patient, asking him to clarify what he meant and reprimanding him for his racist comments. The incident infuriated me, but I had the confidence to challenge his behaviour. Afterwards, I raised it with my manager, and I will never forget her aghast response as she sat there stuttering, not sure what to say or do. I reflected on the fact that so many of my ethnic minority colleagues wouldn't have had the confidence to challenge such behaviour, and this was one of the key incidents that led me to the journey of understanding race equality in the NHS.

The curious questions and sometimes ignorant comments I received from patients and colleagues would leave me questioning how our life experiences were so different. This book was inspired by my own experiences of being witness to racial inequalities, and sometimes being on the receiving end of them too. I am so proud of getting from where I came from to where I am now. It is not lost on me that, at 27 years old, I was the youngest member of senior management teams I worked in, as well as the only Asian in my team, despite the significant under-representation of ethnic minority colleagues we see in the NHS.

There is an intrinsic relationship between healthcare and global events – the NHS itself was born out of post WW2 hardships. More recent events include the murder of George Floyd in the US; Russia's invasion of Ukraine and even the Pride movement which is annually commemorated by NHS Trusts. Following the death of George Floyd, several NHS CEO's wrote to colleagues about the importance of black lives matter and racism. Hundreds were encouraged to seek counselling support and fundraise for Ukraine. With Pride, colleagues are encouraged to attend the Pride festival and talk about their experiences of being LGBT.

In a book about racial inequalities, I would be failing not to mention one of the biggest racial injustices we are witnessing today, along with the failure of NHS organisations in providing support for colleagues affected by this: the plight of the Palestinians. The history of Palestine is considered complex and delicate, however there is no disagreement amongst international law that it is an illegally occupied land, with the UN outlining the right of return for Palestinians refugees since 1957. It is an internationally known (and often largely ignored) fact that the Palestinians have been subjected to theft of land, an apartheid system and a deliberate squeezing of resources, wealth, and the right to live a free life since the occupation began. This has been largely ignored for decades, and following the shocking events of October 7th, a brutal response was unleashed on the Palestinians, tantamount to genocide - as defined by the UN. The killing of healthcare workers; the bombing of 36 hospitals (at the time of writing) and the deliberate starvation of a population in Gaza who has been under siege for almost 20 years. Over 36,000 people have been killed in 8 months, with the majority being children.

The mental and emotional impact on seeing and hearing what is happening in Palestine has had on fellow colleagues I work with in healthcare is increasingly distressing. There has been little to no support, with colleagues reporting they are stifled when attempting to discuss what is happening in Palestine. It shocks me to my core that despite all the work the NHS does for race equality and support for other global causes, the situation in Palestine has been largely silenced, with leaders choosing not to mention it, instead referring to 'global events'. The contrast in how the war in Ukraine and the war in Palestine are observed demonstrates we still have a long way to go when we cannot speak out global injustices happening. It is a telling reminder how even for refugees, the colour of skin matters. For white Ukrainian refugees, we are asked to open our homes, the plight of Ukrainians regularly mentioned in NHS newsletters and communications. When it comes to Palestine, the word is not mentioned, and vague statements about 'conflict in the Middle East' are referred to. Staff are unable to speak freely about how this affects them, with colleagues reporting they are disciplined for speaking about Palestine as it makes others 'uncomfortable'. The fact that a genocide is being live streamed across social media platforms makes me feel incredibly uncomfortable, and the silence surrounding this more so. How can we say we are an employer that champions equity and works to remove inequalities when a genocide is taking place and we remain silent? Fellow healthcare workers being killed and hospitals bombed, and the NHS has unable to express any concern at such events occurring. I therefore dedicate this book to those who struggle and strive for justice, equality and freedom across the globe, and hope for a better future particularly for those who have had to endure such oppression whilst the world remains silent.

I wrote this book because I have met so many fellow people of the global majority who have shared that they felt alone and isolated in their workplace and were struggling to progress or did not know what to do to get to where they wanted to be. When we spoke to each other about our experiences, we realized that we weren't the only ones going through this. The relatability in our experiences of being 'othered' made me realize how little our stories are told. I hope to tell these stories in this book, which you can read as case studies. Furthermore, with knowledge comes action, and therefore I have provided reflective questions for you to consider after each case study.

I never imagined that I would write a book, and I am so grateful for the people who have supported me on this journey. Thank you for taking the time to read this; I hope you find it beneficial. Please do encourage others to read this book too so we can shatter the glass ceiling and unapologetically be who we want to be.

— CHAPTER 1 —

Introduction

The National Health Service. It is a treasure, long envied across the globe, that provides free access to healthcare for all at the point of need. A documentary I recall watching described it as 'the religion of the English people' (Redfish, 2018). Generally, the British people have a love for the NHS, because many of us have benefitted from it at some point in our lives or we know of someone who has. I myself have been fortunate to experience specialist care after a traumatic illness, and I am thankful for the care provided when I sustained a fractured wrist, when my grandfather was terminally ill and when the NHS saved my 18-month-old niece from the devastating effects of encephalomyelitis. There are countless stories of how it has helped people during times of crisis and ill health, and we see daily miracles performed of helping the sick to heal and recover. I can think of hundreds of cases where patients recovered, and we helped them to get better, providing that care and compassion at a worrying time of being tested by ill health.

Where did the NHS begin?
The NHS was born after a period of hardship, poverty and war for the UK. The Second World War had just ended, and although the UK may have been victorious, at home, people were struggling with the after-effects of war and devastation. Many men had died, and many had been injured. As poverty increased, so did illness. Wealth was limited, and people could not afford healthcare, leaving babies and women to die because they could not pay for treatment. The divide between the rich and the poor was evident, manifesting in being able to afford a good quality of life or being burdened with ill health and death.

Although free healthcare for all was initially proposed by the Conservative MP Henry Willink in 1944, it was the Labour Party that implemented it (Brain, 2021). In 1948, Nye Bevan launched the NHS from Park Hospital in Manchester, North West England, with the essential values of helping everyone, providing free healthcare and providing care based on need rather than ability to pay (Campbell, 2016). To this day, the first point of the NHS constitution states that the service is for all, regardless of gender, disability, age, sexual orientation, religion, belief, gender reassignment, pregnancy, maternity, marital or civil partnership status and race (Department of Health and Social Care, 2023). It further states that the NHS has a wider social duty to promote equality through the services it provides and to pay particular attention to groups or sections of society where improvements are not keeping pace with the rest of the population. I highlight this point of the constitution, as the reader should bear this in mind when it comes to discussing racial inequalities in this book.

Fast forward to the 21st century and despite many challenges, problems and even a global pandemic, the NHS remains. It continues to provide free healthcare amongst a concerning backdrop of chronic underfunding, high numbers of staff leaving and increasing demand on overstretched services. On average, over 1.6 million interactions occur daily across the NHS, consisting of GP appointments, community visits, outpatient appointments, inpatient stays, accident and emergency (A&E) attendance and calls to NHS Direct (111 service) and ambulance services (Bulut, 2023). It is, therefore, a very busy system. Over 1.2 million people are employed by the NHS, making it the largest employer in Europe (NHS Digital, 2022). In total, 25.7 per cent of the NHS workforce is from a black, Asian or minority ethnic (BAME) background, making it one of the largest employers of BAME people in the country. This proportion is high, especially when compared with the overall UK population, where BAME people make up 18 per cent (Diversity UK, 2023). Compared with other sectors of employment, there is a high proportion of BAME people working in healthcare. But little is understood about their experiences, despite racial inequalities featuring regularly as an issue that the NHS faces. In this book, I will highlight the experiences of BAME people in the NHS.

BAME people in the UK

The UK has a colourful relationship with people of BAME backgrounds. The families of most of us who were born in the UK come from other countries, and we are therefore the diaspora. We were born here, we live, work and study here, but sometimes we may feel we don't belong, even though this country is the place we call home. There are various factors that contribute to this, some of which are relevant to this book. These include the lack of representation in mainstream society, marginalization of BAME people from mainstream society and discrimination (Ethnic Dimension, 2014). I will discuss what this looks like in later chapters.

When it comes to politics, we have seen some improvement at least in relation to skin colour, witnessing not one but two of the highest offices in the land being filled by British Asian men: the first being British Indian Prime Minister, Rishi Sunak, and the second being British Pakistani former First Minister of Scotland, Humza Yousaf. Sunak rose to power after the messy internal politics of the ruling Conservative party led to his predecessor resigning after just 45 days in the role. Although it is significant to see a BAME person become prime minister, this is not the experience or reality for most people across the UK. Most BAME people sadly come from deprived backgrounds, stuck in a cycle of poverty that is perpetuated through existing societal inequalities (Butler, 2022). Most are not from the same background as someone like Rishi Sunak, i.e., a multimillionaire.

The right-wing narrative about minorities that is peddled by the government exacerbates negative attitudes towards them, leading some of us to question our place in British society, where we are 'othered' and made to feel unwelcome in our own country. The particularly aggressive anti-immigration policies that were proposed under the former home secretary Suella Braverman contributed to an increasingly hostile environment for people of colour, particularly those who are vulnerable, such as asylum seekers and refugees. This was evidenced by a firebomb attack on a migrant centre in Dover in October 2022 and violent scenes in Knowsley in March 2023 (Taylor, 2023). An article by Taylor (2023) noted a clear warning to politicians to refrain from the use of inflammatory rhetoric, which is contributing to stirring up hatred amongst the different communities of the UK. This provides a backdrop to the setting of the UK in which the

NHS operates within British society. Racial dynamics play an increasing role in how we operate as a society and therefore how systems within that society operate, for example, the healthcare system.

BAME people and employment

In employment, the Race at Work (UK Government, 2018) report states that just 38 per cent of employees are comfortable talking about race at work. In the NHS, one in four BAME employees reported witnessing or experiencing racist harassment or bullying from managers in the last two years (NHS England, 2023). In total, 30.3 per cent of BAME NHS staff reported experiencing harassment, bullying or abuse from patients, relatives or the public, a higher percentage than their white counterparts (NHS England, 2023). Despite there being a higher proportion of BAME employees (25%) in the NHS compared to other sectors, they are over-represented in lower paid roles. These higher risk groups are often in frontline care roles, like healthcare assistant, cleaner and junior nursing roles.

There is a lack of BAME individuals in senior or leadership positions in the NHS. The effect of this is that services may not encompass the needs of communities that are not represented in decision-making. Now, I am not saying that BAME people must necessarily be in leadership positions to eliminate this, as having someone of colour in a senior position wouldn't simply eradicate the issue. However, having had all-white boards and leadership teams since the formation of the NHS clearly hasn't done much to acknowledge racism in healthcare, let alone manage it. This was evident during the Covid-19 pandemic, when the issue of disproportionate impact on BAME communities was prevalent. During this time, however, communities were scapegoated for the rise of Covid-19, with the claim that BAME people were 'not taking [the pandemic] seriously enough' (BBC, 2020), despite evidence showing white middle-class communities were demonstrating lower levels of compliance with the social distancing rules.

BAME and Covid-19

BAME colleagues felt left behind and unheard during the Covid-19 pandemic; for example, working in nursing and healthcare roles but not being provided with personal protective equipment (PPE), being forced to work shifts so that other staff could work non-clinically and avoid being exposed to the virus and not receiving vital information to understand how to respond to the pandemic. I recall meeting with BAME staff who were concerned about raising issues because they felt that no one understood how the Covid-19 pandemic felt for them.

The book will detail the importance of representation in later chapters, but to simplify it here: how do you serve a people you know very little about? Not accommodating for or understanding cultural needs or nuance provides a poorer experience in the workplace. It leads to decisions that do not necessarily benefit under-represented communities and can lead to furthering inequalities. It can have a detrimental effect on patient safety and patient care, as discussed throughout this book. The differences in how communities respond to health in the UK became drastically apparent during the Covid-19 pandemic, when BAME communities were disproportionately impacted by the disease in terms of prevalence, physiological impact and the number of deaths (the rate of BAME people dying of Covid-19 was far higher than that of white people) (Platt and Warwick, 2020).

Disproportionate impact may be a term we have become desensitized to, but the reality looks like this: family members losing the only person who helped them survive; a mother losing her son; a young wife with children now a widow, mourning not only the loss of her loved one but also the loss of income, making it harder to cope. We have little appreciation of how Covid-19 impacted people of different cultures in the UK, because most of our institutions do not appreciate or understand how people live differently. For example, in Asian culture, it is common to see multigenerational households being used to maintain stronger family and cultural ties than in other communities in the UK. But during the Covid-19 pandemic, this meant some older family members were at higher risk of contracting Covid-19 due to younger family members working in key roles.

Understanding cultural differences and appreciating how parts of the population perceive and respond to healthcare translates to a better patient experience when interacting with healthcare services. Under-represented populations are better understood when their presence is reflected in leadership that represents them and their communities. This links to a theme we commonly hear of 'diversity in leadership', with one of the benefits being relatability to patient populations. Being able to understand and connect to populations means the NHS can better respond as a resilient service to meet the diverse needs of populations we serve. This is well documented in research, but how have we come to the point of knowing this, and parroting it, but seeing little change?

BAME and discrimination in the NHS

Discrimination and lack of cultural understanding remain rife. This is exacerbated by poor BAME representation in senior leadership, which is reflective of the institutional racism that exists within the NHS (Kline and Martin, 2013). Anecdotally, before 2015, BAME NHS employees reported feeling that they were being treated in a worse way than their white counterparts, but this information was not measured. The introduction of the Workforce Race Equality Standard (WRES) for NHS trusts changed this, since trusts were mandated to collect data relating to indicators affecting BAME staff. Whilst there has been some improvement, the NHS Staff Survey still highlights higher rates of discrimination and fewer career progression opportunities for BAME staff than their white counterparts (West, 2020).

The higher rates of discrimination, lower representation at senior levels of leadership and fewer career progression opportunities experienced by BAME colleagues paints a bleak picture. And it begs the question: what do we do to change this to provide equitable opportunities for all? I am a firm believer that where there is a will, there is a way. So I hope that sharing the experiences of others in this book will shed light on this issue, provide food for thought and support us to break the 'glass ceiling' that many of us look up through.

The purpose of the book

The impetus for this book came from witnessing and experiencing discrimination in the NHS. Statistically, I am someone who will face the 'triple discrimination' penalty within British society: 1) being female; 2) being Asian; 3) hijab wearing and therefore being a visible

Muslim. This means I am more likely to be questioned about my family life plans than white female counterparts, less likely to be given a job compared with the rest of the British population and more likely to be paid less (Muslim Engagement and Development, 2017). It seems that many of us view the dream of career progression through a glass ceiling, meaning we get to a certain point and then can't go any higher for unexplained reasons.

But is having BAME leaders important? Throughout history, leaders have risen to stand up for others, change the status quo, end oppression and establish justice. We look up to such people because they dare to stand apart from others. And that is not always easy to do. It takes courage to stand up. It requires important skills and traits, like being prepared and able to sacrifice your time and being persistent in your efforts, and you must develop attributes like self-belief, compassion and commitment. Although it is easy to use such words to describe leadership, it is the consistency with which these qualities are applied that truly distinguishes a leader from others.

Sometimes we can be fearful of leadership. Questions like, 'Is leadership something someone like me is capable of doing?' can be asked. As a woman of colour and faith, I have had times of doubting myself, as I am sure many others do too. It was not until I engaged with other leaders that I realized that these fears can be quite normal. You will never truly know everything, and this is best managed by having a mindset of curiosity and constantly learning. Seeking and practising knowledge means you are more confident in making decisions, because you accept that you might not always know the best way but are willing to learn as things unfold. It gives you confidence in going to ask other people who may know and in then making informed judgements and decisions. It is important to establish links with people who can provide sound advice and judgement. Having a critical eye and mindset with the confidence to challenge thoughts/ideas can steer decision-making during times of difficulty.

When does one decide to become a leader? And is a leader a manager? Some people believe that certain people have a natural talent for leadership and others rise to the top in the face of setbacks. I recall speaking at a leadership programme aimed at BAME nurses in the NHS. During my talk, I spoke about failure, which we are sometimes conditioned to be afraid of, and its importance.

A lady interrupted me to say that it is disheartening to go through failure again and again. It's what made her give up, because she knew that the system was rigged – favouring less-experienced, white colleagues for the next promotion instead of her 20 years' experience. She expressed that this felt unfair, especially when she was asked to support the training needs of the new senior staff, despite her being told she was 'not experienced enough' for the same role. It caused hurt and frustration at the barriers that were being put in the way of her progression. Her feelings of loneliness led to despondency, crushing her ambitions to succeed in her career, and she felt terribly alone as she watched other colleagues progress and thrive. Whilst she felt alone, though, she wasn't. This is a common scenario amongst BAME people, as we shall see from the stories of those who have contributed to this book. It was this incident that led me to reflect on how little our experiences as BAME individuals are heard, inspiring me to write this book to share our voices.

Earlier I touched on why representation of BAME people in leadership is important for supporting services designed to meet the needs of all communities. However, it serves a further purpose of supporting BAME colleagues who require support from the leadership system. An example of this took place during the Covid-19 pandemic, where BAME colleagues were dying disproportionately, which had a psychological and emotional impact on those who were aware of this. I recall a junior colleague of mine at the time, a physiotherapist, contacting me to express her fears that she could be more at risk from the virus, especially after working in intensive care and seeing that most patients being treated were either black or Asian. She reported colleagues' whispers stating that, 'Covid seems to kill more BAME people than others,' but no one addressed how this might impact her as an Asian member of staff or whether any measures were being taken to support her.

As I escalated this through senior channels, it became apparent that this was a national issue and was being responded to far too slowly. BAME staff were worried and felt that there was little representation and few people in leadership roles to whom they could express their concerns. The co-chair of the BAME network I chaired at the time and I were successful in delivering a risk assessment for BAME colleagues, as well as leading a webinar on what managers could do to provide support during this time. The trust's CEO held a webinar to listen to the concerns of BAME staff to try and support meaningful change. I will never forget the words of a Filipino nurse who shared that he did not feel comfortable raising his fears with his senior colleagues because they did not understand his concerns. This is one of the reasons why representation is so important.

As the NHS continues to evolve and develop for the future, so does the ambition of how it represents everyone in society, particularly those who are disadvantaged or under-represented. Statistics show that the highest number of Emergency Department attendees tend to be from deprived backgrounds (Giebel *et al.*, 2019). It cannot be denied that one of the many causes of this is the lack of awareness of services. This is often because services are not tailored to the requirements of different communities or because the link between services and those who need them most simply isn't there.

A common phrase I hear in leadership circles when referring to under-represented communities is 'hard-to-reach' communities. But why are they hard to reach? When we as a healthcare system are here to serve everyone, regardless of race, gender, background, etc., how are we not reaching everyone? It is reassuring that the language used is slowly changing to 'yet-to-reach' communities; however, the implicit understanding that we are not able to engage effectively with such communities despite their higher use of services compared with other groups is a problem. This indicates that we have communities that are not represented but we are not engaging with them effectively to support their health needs.

I wanted this book to highlight the stories of various BAME people I interviewed and to share their experiences with others. I also interviewed people working in the NHS who are white to share their experiences and interactions with race equality and provide greater understanding of this topic in which we all have a role to play. I have provided these stories in a case-study format with reflective questions to provide practical learning points for the reader to take action on. Names indicated with an * have been changed along with other identifying characteristics in order to ensure anonymity.

Before continuing, it is important to address the use of the term 'BAME' when describing people of black, Asian or minority ethnic background. It is not a term I prefer to use, and it comes with some controversy. 'BAME' does not highlight the rich cultural identities that exist within the various ethnic groups that make up this term. However, its use is unfortunately widespread in the NHS. For the sake of ease, I have used it throughout this book, but it is important to highlight that there are various terms to describe people. Some people do not feel comfortable with this term at all, some use 'global majority' and some use 'ethnic minority'. As for which term is 'best', it is not for me to determine, but rather, it is incumbent on each person to identify how they wish to be referred to and for allies and others to ask how people prefer to be referred to. I hope you find this beneficial, whichever stage of the journey you are on.

— CHAPTER 2 —

Racial Inequalities

Since its inception in 1947, the NHS has relied upon immigrants to sustain its delivery, longevity and success in delivering free healthcare for all. When the UK was attempting to rebuild itself after the Second World War, there wasn't enough manpower to sustain public services. The UK therefore called upon the people of Commonwealth countries to come to the UK for employment in exchange for UK citizenship. And come they did. People moved here from the Caribbean and Asia, taking up work in factories, rebuilding the country and sustaining the development of the newly formed NHS by taking on roles to support the delivery of the health system. This generation became known as the Windrush generation, and without their intervention, the NHS would not have survived or been sustainable.

The Windrush generation left behind their lives in their home countries, invited by the UK to come and work. In 2018, the Windrush generation were terribly mistreated following a political scandal in which citizens were wrongly deported by the UK Home Office. A huge backlash and criticism of the scandal followed, forcing the government to hold the Windrush inquiry, which concluded that the scandal was both 'foreseeable and avoidable' and therefore need not have occurred (Williams, 2018).

Whilst the Windrush generation mainly comprises those of Caribbean descent, the UK's Commonwealth is much larger than this and includes Southeast Asia. As a result, many South Asians also migrated here; again, at the invitation of the British, who were providing Commonwealth citizens with indefinite leave to remain in the UK (Lowe, 2020). It is interesting to compare this time with today: the UK once openly welcomed immigrants to live and work here, in comparison with the current hostile, anti-immigrant policies in which vulnerable people are shipped off to other countries.

Despite this long history, there has historically been little representation of BAME people in leadership or senior management in the NHS. The rumbles of racism and being treated differently because you were not white were prevalent, but little changed. Many Caribbean healthcare assistants reported that despite being trained as nurses in their home countries, they were not supported to continue nursing in the UK or encouraged to aspire to reach higher levels of training or employment. They worked as auxiliaries or healthcare assistants, despite being overqualified and underpaid for the skills they had (Ali, 2021).

The history of race equality in the NHS

In 2004, the Department of Health developed a Race Equality Action Plan designed to tackle racial discrimination for both service users and employees (Strategic Health Authority, 2004). The main actions from the plan for BAME populations were to meet people's service needs, support with high incidence of chronic disease and improve recruitment opportunities. Ten years on, little has changed, with anecdotal reports of racism in the NHS still prevalent.

Roger Kline – a long-standing advocate for race equality in healthcare – carried out a survey examining race discrimination in NHS leadership (Kline, 2014). Prior to Kline's report, a body of evidence was available that linked staff satisfaction to good patient care, and showed disproportionate favouring of white applicants in the interview process and little to no representation of BAME people in leadership positions. Kline's report focused on BAME representation in NHS trusts, and therefore did not include primary care and clinical commissioning groups (now replaced with Integrated Care Boards (ICBs)). Both services make up a significant portion of the healthcare system, and therefore, future research should include these to ensure there is an understanding across the wider healthcare system of race equality. What Kline's report does offer is a stark insight into race equality in the NHS as far back as 2013.

In 2013, BAME board representation in London was just 8 per cent. In a city known for its diversity, with 45 per cent of the population and 41 per cent of NHS trust staff being BAME, it is startling that such little BAME representation was present in leadership positions – and this has remained unchanged since 2007. Between 2008 and 2013, there was little change nationally in BAME leadership representation at senior and very senior management (VSM) level, remaining at around 5.5 per cent over five years. There was no increase noted in the proportion of BAME nurse directors in the ten years from 2003 to 2013. This leads one to question how effective the Department of Health's Race Equality Action Plan was at the time and to question why people of BAME background were not progressing in their careers.

When reviewing BAME representation across service regulators and the board of NHS England, the picture is no different. In 2014, NHS England had 2 out of 14 directors who were BAME, whilst the service regulatory bodies at the time (NHS Trust Development Authority (NHS TDA), Monitor, Care Quality Commission (CQC) and Professional Standards Authority for Health and Social Care (PSA), which have since merged) had no BAME representation. It is worth noting that the two directors in NHS England who were BAME were non-executives, meaning no executive directors (who have voting rights on boards) were BAME. Kline suggested that the poor leadership representation at national level translated to a failure in representative leadership at local level.

The impact of under-representation

Poor BAME representation in leadership makes it challenging to ensure that care meets the requirements of different communities that exist within a population. Without an understanding of different communities and challenges they face, it is difficult to tailor services to what is needed, which impacts patient care. How do you best serve populations if you have little understanding of the nuances of different cultures and experiences? Research demonstrates that BAME staff generally have a poorer experience in the workplace, consisting of: fewer career opportunities; discrimination from colleagues, managers and patients; and not feeling valued in the workplace. This correlates with patient experience and patient safety, because if staff do not have the confidence to approach their managers with an issue relating to patients, this impacts the patient experience, potentially contributing to patient safety issues.

An example of this is a doctor who may be concerned that a patient is deteriorating, but due to feeling undermined and victimized by their manager, they feel reluctant to raise a concern about the patient. Not feeling psychologically safe to raise concerns could lead to them feeling unable to speak up. If the patient is deteriorating, this could lead to serious illness or even death, with a contributing factor being the doctor not feeling confident to speak up due to feeling targeted by their manager. The reasons for staff feeling this way should be evaluated; reasons might include not feeling supported or valued or there not being an open and respecting workplace culture. There are multiple factors that would influence a scenario like this; however, racism can be a contributing factor, and it is one that remains unchanged despite significant debate.

The Francis report highlighted trusts' responsibility to ensure there is a culture in which staff feel supported when speaking up and are supported to raise concerns (Francis, 2013). The question is, though: if someone feels targeted because of their culture, faith or race being 'othered' in the workplace, then how confident are they going to be to speak up? It is a challenge to do this, and this is demonstrated throughout the case studies in this book.

Kline's report highlighted the significance of discrimination and race inequalities, challenging the lack of BAME people in leadership. It was a groundbreaking report that shined a light on an issue that was well known but conventionally brushed under the carpet. It brought the issue of racism in UK healthcare to light, paving the way for further work to improve race equality in the NHS. Race inequalities are historical and remain prevalent in society, with recent examples including the disproportionate impact of Covid-19 on BAME people, the murder of George Floyd in the US and the 2022 Shattered Hopes report that shined a light on BAME inequalities in the NHS. Inequalities often stem from discrimination, and before we discuss and analyse the impact of racial inequalities, it is important to define racial discrimination so we can understand the root cause.

Racial discrimination

Racial discrimination is the act of being treated differently because of your race. This could be a single action, a repetitive one or even the result of policy based on race. It may or may not be intentional, but either way it is unlawful as per the Equality Act 2010 (Equality and Human Rights Commission, 2020).

The Equality Act 2010 is legislation that was introduced to remove discrimination of marginalized groups to ensure equality. It outlines nine characteristics that are to be protected in the workplace:

- Race
- Age
- Gender reassignment
- Sexual orientation
- Marriage and civil partnership
- Pregnancy and maternity
- Disability
- Religion or belief
- Gender

   (UK Government, 2010)

Discrimination can be experienced in various ways. The Advisory, Conciliation and Arbitration Service (Acas) – the UK's independent public body that provides employment advice and guidance – states that there are four types of racial discrimination: direct, indirect, harassment and victimization, each of which can be experienced differently as well as simultaneously (Acas, 2023).

Examples of racial discrimination are discussed in later chapters of this book. It is important to understand that discrimination of any kind leads to inequalities, and several reports have been released over the years that highlight this. In 2016, the Equality and Human Rights Commission (EHRC) identified five urgent areas where racial inequalities demanded action: education, crime, health, living standards and employment. Unemployment was significantly higher for ethnic minorities (12.9%) than for white people (6.3%); black people were earning 23.1 per cent less on average than white people – even when they had university degrees; a significantly lower percentage of ethnic minorities were working in management roles, as identified earlier in this chapter (Equality and Human Rights Commission, 2016).

When it comes to crime, rates of prosecution and sentencing for black people were three times higher than for white people (*ibid.*). Ethnic minorities were more likely to be victims of murder and race hate crimes in the country.

Living standards for BAME people were generally lower and poorer. For example, the EHRC report stated that Pakistani, Bangladeshi and black adults were more likely to live in substandard accommodation than white people. Ethnic minorities were also more likely to live in poverty – at a rate of 35.7 per cent compared with just 17.2 per cent of white people (*ibid.*).

In relation to healthcare, the EHRC report stated that a significantly disproportionate number of people of ethnic minorities were detained under mental health legislation in hospitals in England and Wales; poorer mental health was found in Gypsy, Traveller and Roma communities than in the rest of the population. Further, black women were *seven times* more likely to be detained than white women (*ibid.*).

The above provides a bleak picture of racial inequalities in the UK, and it is concerning that these are statistics from 2016. The situation remains the same nearly ten years on. Since this report, the UK has seen seismic events that have deepened polarization amongst the UK's communities, like Brexit, the Covid-19 pandemic and the refugee 'crisis', all of which have significantly highlighted or exacerbated racial inequalities.

In 2021, the Commission on Race and Ethnic Disparities (CRED) published its race report, laying bare the existing racial inequalities in healthcare for patients. The report highlights that maternal deaths are *five times higher* for black mothers and twice as high for Asian mothers compared with mothers from white ethnic backgrounds. In Scotland, avoidable hospital admissions were higher amongst Pakistanis than white communities, potentially suggesting issues in accessing primary care or early intervention. The report further highlights the impact of Covid-19, acknowledging that black men were three times more likely to die from Covid-19 in the first wave than their white counterparts. When it comes to mental health, the commission highlights findings from the Wessely review that black people were eight times more likely to be subjected to community treatment orders than white people and four times more likely to be detained (Wessely, 2018).

It is interesting, and rather disconcerting, to note that evidence of differences between the experience of BAME patients and white patients existed even nearly 20 years ago. This was evident in both primary care and hospital patient surveys (Healthcare Commission, 2009). In 2021, Watkinson led a cross-sectional study reviewing experiences of older people, which found the same issue of prevalent racial inequalities. This included poor experiences of primary care, insufficient support from local services, low self-confidence in patients managing their own health conditions and high social deprivation compared with the white British group (Watkinson, Sutton and Turner, 2021).

Whilst the CRED report highlights some of the racial inequalities that BAME people experience, it was refuted by the British Medical Association (BMA), despite it providing key evidence to the commission. The BMA highlighted that the report failed to define racism and failed to acknowledge the role of structural racism and its impact on UK citizens. This is despite the presence of structural racism in the UK being recognized internationally, as per the UN Special Rapporteur on racism in 2018 (BMA, 2021).

Experiencing racial inequalities can generally be said to lead to a poorer life experience. Having good health is indeed a privilege, a blessing. Imagine that you are unwell and unable to go about your daily business because of ill health. Now imagine that, in the context of the above examples, you are more exposed to disease (like ethnic minorities were at the height of the Covid-19 pandemic) or you are not able to access the healthcare required due to language barriers or because you don't know where to go to get help. Perhaps when you do access it, you have a significantly poorer experience and are told your symptoms are 'in your head' or you are simply not believed by the healthcare professional. It is a problem that continues, despite being well documented over the years by reports, surveys and analysis from various healthcare bodies.

When it comes to staff and racial inequalities, we see a dire picture in terms of job satisfaction, morale, career progression and leadership representation. People are reluctant to voice their experiences of the systemic racism they face at work, perhaps for fear of it not being acknowledged or of being further isolated because they raised a concern. NHS trusts have introduced Freedom to Speak Up Guardians, attempting to encourage people to raise concerns in a safe and non-judgemental manner. However, cases of clear discrimination still occur, leaving staff feeling isolated, alone and discriminated against and thereby not able to perform as well as they can or should. One such case in 2012 was that of Elliot Browne, who was awarded £1 million in damages from a Manchester NHS trust after experiencing race discrimination. When one considers the amount of financial damage, reputational damage, use of resources to manage the tribunal and time taken away from the clinical setting to investigate this situation, as well as the impact on the individual, it is a considerable cost to public health services. In this case, race discrimination was denied by the trust's board, which subsequently denied there was racism in the workplace, even after the unanimous decision that racial discrimination had occurred was made by the tribunal (Furness, 2012).

Racial inequalities and health: sickle cell disease

The relevance of racial equality when it comes to service provision is evident in illnesses that are 'more prevalent' amongst BAME populations, such as sickle cell disease, which is poorly understood. A historiography reviewing sickle cell disease highlights the lack of equitable provision of sickle cell services in the UK, dating back to 1973 (Redhead, 2021). A poignant point in Redhead's research is the long-standing contradiction at the heart of public services in the UK: they were founded on and supported by migrant populations who have since faced exclusion from the very services they have built.

In 2013, a major peer review of services in the UK for patients with sickle cell disease found that only a fifth of services had adequate numbers of staff with the right skills. The national coordinator at the UK Thalassemia Society at the time stated that, 'If these conditions affected the white mainstream population rather than ethnic minority communities, perhaps they wouldn't be so badly overlooked' (Kline, 2014). The Sickle Cell Society CEO told the *Health Service Journal* (HSJ) that race was a factor in the equity of services across the UK and that patients with the disease appeared to be neglected in high prevalence areas (Calkin, 2013). Ten years later, research continues to be conducted reviewing sickle cell patients' experiences of barriers to treatment, and it is still widely misunderstood, thereby impacting patient experience, particularly in acute episodes of the disease (White, 2022). This work is currently being undertaken by the Race and Health Observatory in collaboration with Mind, the mental health charity.

Other services where there is significant difference in the experience of BAME patients are mental health, maternity and cancer services. In 2006, ministers acknowledged that BAME service users were being discriminated against unlawfully and unethically in mental health services (Dent, 2006). Since then, UK legislation has introduced the Equality Act 2010 to tackle racial inequalities; however, the impact of this remains to be seen, as little change has been reported in equity of services for BAME people. A briefing by the mental health charity Mind highlights the inequalities for BAME people in accessing mental health services in England (Mind, 2020). These include being more likely to access treatment through the criminal justice system, four times more likely to be sectioned and three times more likely to be subjected to 'restrictive interventions' such as being restrained or isolated whilst in hospital. When it comes to receiving treatment, BAME populations are less likely to complete a full course of intervention and less likely to achieve full recovery than their white counterparts. Mind recognizes the issues of higher prevalence of mental health problems in some communities, as well as how racism can affect mental health. One of its key recommendations for improving racial inequalities in mental health is to include the provision of culturally competent and relevant community services to support early intervention. It is also interesting to note that while instances of mental health problems amongst BAME populations are high in the UK, in Asia and Africa, rates are much lower, which begs the question: what is happening in the UK amongst such populations that contributes to poorer mental health? A possibility is the systemic and institutional racism that impacts daily life, progression and job or life satisfaction, preventing one from being able to live without prejudice or judgement.

Racial inequalities and maternity

Inequalities in maternity services have seen significant media coverage, with the MBRRACE-UK report being addressed in Parliament, since black and Asian women (as well as babies) are significantly more likely to die during childbirth than their white counterparts (Knight *et al.*, 2022). Whilst this report rightfully received significant attention, the picture of maternity services exhibiting racial disparity in patient experience is historical. Almost ten years before the MBRRACE-UK report was released, the Public Accounts Committee found that BAME mothers reported fewer positive patient experiences and were significantly more likely to report shortfalls in choice and continuity of care. This led the committee to conclude that NHS maternity services had failed BAME mothers by not 'address[ing] persistent inequalities in maternity care' (Public Accounts Committee, 2014).

Racial inequalities and cancer

Some types of cancer (prostate cancer, mouth cancer and breast cancer) are more prevalent amongst BAME communities, as are late diagnoses and poorer survival rates (Thomson and Forman, 2009). Over ten years later, the picture remains the same. The Race Equality Foundation detailed higher incidence of certain cancers in BAME communities, poorer experiences in BAME populations of cancer care and a poor understanding in healthcare services of the needs of BAME communities (Fazil, 2018). Its report details a lack of cultural competence education for health providers and shows clear evidence that the management of healthcare is not being treated with the focus, priority or urgency that a disease like cancer requires in BAME populations.

It is clear from the above that discrimination (in its various forms) has an impact on patient care, as concluded by West, Dawson and Kaur (2015). Cultural incompetence, a lack of awareness and understanding, and a lack of representation are all factors linked to this. A further interesting link impacting clinical outcomes is staff treatment. West's research showed that the most consistently strongly linked factor to patient survey scores was discrimination, particularly racial discrimination. The research demonstrated a clear link between discrimination and aggression against staff, and patient satisfaction. West concluded that the greater the proportion of BAME staff reporting discrimination in the previous 12 months, the lower the levels of patient satisfaction, arguing:

> the experience of BME staff is a very good barometer of the climate of respect and care for all within NHS Trusts...put simply, if BME staff feel engaged, motivated, valued and part of a team with a sense of belonging, patients were more likely to be satisfied with the service they received. (West et al., 2012, cited in Kline, 2014)

Evidence suggests that less discrimination stimulates greater innovation and performance, as evidenced in boards that had 50 per cent female membership, which performed better than boards that did not have female membership (Chambers et al., 2011). When people can see others who look like them, they are inspired to be able to communicate with those people if they feel they can approach them with the understanding that they will be heard and understood. [AQ] Earlier I mentioned attending a webinar that was held during the Covid-19 pandemic so the CEO of the trust I worked with could listen to BAME staff concerns following the disproportionate impact of the disease on them. I will never forget a Filipino nurse who raised his hand to share his fears of working on the ward without PPE while feeling too worried to raise his concerns with his management. When asked why, he looked tired, fearful and stressed. His response was that he could not see anyone in management who looked like him who would understand his concerns. However, the webinar had a panel of black, Asian and white people, so he felt he could raise his voice with the panel.

Imagine if this individual had felt able to raise his concerns with his matron and felt well supported and understood in the workplace. We probably would not have had to spend hours planning and leading webinars and meetings to listen to staff and provide a psychologically safe space to raise concerns. We could have reduced staff anxiety levels, which were heightened at the time because of the disproportionate impact Covid-19 was having on our colleagues, and we likely would have supported better patient care, as staff would not have needed time away from wards to attend the webinars. Whilst the webinar was worth hosting because of the support it gave staff who were struggling, my argument is that had we had representative leadership that led effectively, understood people's cultural backgrounds and concerns, and provided staff with a sense of belonging, they may have then felt better supported and able to continue their roles with more confidence. Inequalities have an impact.

The cost of racial inequalities

The Marmot review (Marmot, 2010) suggests that inequality costs the healthcare system over £36–40 billion through lost taxes, welfare payments and costs to the NHS. Whilst it is ambitious to suggest that fixing inequality will fix the chronic underfunding and wider issues surrounding the NHS, it is not ambitious to suggest that tackling the inequalities will make a difference. One would expect that fixing inequalities would result in a better, responsive healthcare service that meets the needs of all, as well as incurring financial benefits. It is also important to note that inequalities are not applicable only in a racial context; other populations at risk of inequalities include women, people of religion and those of certain sexual orientations. Between the different characteristics exists an intersectionality, as identities can be made up of multiple characteristics. For example, a young Muslim woman who is black potentially faces more inequalities due to the various characteristics of being a woman, a person of faith and her race than a white male of no faith.

Research supports the view that diverse climates lead to improved performance, decreased absenteeism and greater customer satisfaction (Hofhuis, van der Rijt and Vlug, 2016). The staff and organizational benefit for the NHS is clear. From a service perspective, Ashikali, Groeneveld and Kuipers (2021) found that the ethnic representativeness of a workforce has an influence on the perception of service users, and thereby organizational performance. Upon reading this study, I wondered whether this could be one of the reasons why there was a reluctance amongst BAME communities to seek healthcare assistance during the Covid-19 pandemic. Whilst a higher number of BAME people were being admitted to hospitals during the

Covid-19 pandemic, the messaging and media communications were initially predominantly white. This begs the question raised earlier, of: how can communities be served when they are not represented in the system? The same questions and opinions arise when addressing racial inequalities in healthcare, which makes me wonder: is it so difficult that we just can't do it, or is it simple but the willingness to make the change just isn't there? Amongst the backdrop of the society we live in, it feels challenging to address this pertinent issue. Not doing so means the issues remain and inequalities continue, and nobody really benefits from this.

The introduction of the WRES

Being able to measure indicators affecting race equality helps us to understand the problem, which is why Simon Stevens, former CEO of NHS England, unveiled the WRES tool after the Kline report in 2014. This was one attempt to propel the NHS towards seriously addressing race equality by expecting all NHS organizations to report on race-related data.

The WRES tool is now mandated across all NHS trusts, but other than at board level and in HR departments, little is known about this standard across the various management layers in the NHS. It is important that management levels understand this workforce standard so they can locally implement and understand its indicators. Whilst the WRES may be led by equality, diversity and inclusion (EDI) leads, it is not solely their responsibility. It is the responsibility of all managers to ensure EDI is supported in the workplace. The WRES measures nine standards, called the race equality indicators. These are as follows:

1. Percentage of black and minority ethnic staff.

2. Relative likelihood of white applicants being appointed from shortlisting across all posts compared with BME applicants.

3. Relative likelihood of BME staff entering the formal disciplinary process compared with white staff.

4. Relative likelihood of white staff accessing non-mandatory

training and continuing professional development (CPD) compared with BME staff.

5. Percentage of staff experiencing bullying, harassment or abuse from patients, relatives or the public in the last 12 months.

6. Percentage of staff experiencing bullying, harassment or abuse from staff in the last 12 months.

7. Percentage of staff believing that the trust provides equal opportunities for career progression or promotion.

8. Percentage of staff personally experiencing discrimination at work from a manager/team leader or other colleagues.

9. BME board membership.

(WRES, 2022)

Collecting data to be able to analyse it effectively takes time; however, eight years on, we are seeing trends in the data. From 2016 to 2022, there was an increase in the number of BAME staff working in the NHS from 17.7 per cent to 24.2 per cent (NHS England, 2022). Representation at VSM level has almost doubled from 5.4 per cent to 10.3 per cent. Board membership (this is different to VSM level, as it is made up of executive or non-executive directors) has increased from 7.1 per cent to 13.2 per cent (NHS Quality and Diversity Council, 2017). Progress is being made in terms of representation, but there is little change in other indicators, such as BAME staff experiencing bullying, harassment or abuse from patients, relatives and the public (indicator 5) or from staff (indicator 6), or experiencing discrimination at work (indicator 8). BAME staff still report that trusts are not providing equal opportunities for career progression or promotion; in fact, they report that opportunities are significantly lower for them than for their white counterparts.

It is astonishing that over 70 years after BAME people came to support the healthcare system, progress is still ongoing, only really taking place in the last ten years or so – since the WRES was introduced. We still hear horrific stories of racism limiting career opportunities and impacting health and wellbeing. Reports are regularly released on this topic, and the impact of inequalities is regularly examined. But what does this mean for individuals? How does this impact the person experiencing them? There is little opportunity to hear first-hand the lived experience of those it impacts the most, and therefore this book provides a voice for the untold stories in the form of case studies for the reader to benefit and learn from.

— CHAPTER 3 —

Case Study 1: Allied Health Professions

This chapter will discuss:

- the role of occupational therapists (OTs) and allied health professionals (AHPs)
- BAME representation in allied health professions
- microaggressions: the definition, examples and impact
- the importance of language, understanding and representation.

This case study focuses on an OT's experience of working in the NHS. OTs have a key yet often undervalued role in supporting patients' independence and function post illness. Particularly in acute secondary care settings, OTs support patients to go home safely by providing equipment, understanding care needs and supporting them to be safe and independent at home.

Allied health professionals

Occupational therapy is one of the 14 professions that fall under the banner of 'allied health professions': physiotherapists, OTs, dieticians, speech and language therapists, podiatrists, art therapists, drama therapists, music therapists, operating department practitioners, orthoptists, osteopaths, paramedics, prosthetists and orthotists, and radiographers (NHS England, n.d.). In recent years, AHPs have focused on increasing awareness of the roles they fulfil, in part because of the underappreciation and limited awareness of the roles they have in supporting health and wellbeing.

The starting salary range for most AHPs is band 5 at £28,408 (NHS Employers, 2022). Particularly in professions like occupational therapy, physiotherapy, speech and language therapy, and dietetics, professionals will work at junior level for around two years and then progress to a senior role. This is dependent on skill, exposure to different environments and experience. Some may progress in 18 months, and others may take longer. Confidence, competence and support with career progression all affect the amount of time it takes AHPs to progress.

Band 6 roles are generally senior AHP roles, where one starts to increase one's responsibility for managing complex caseloads, deliver training to junior colleagues and deputize for the senior specialist, which means assuming more managerial tasks. The next progression is to a band 7 role, which means managing a team of AHPs and being responsible and accountable to the service lead. Band 7s are responsible for the training and development of the team and must respond to any incidents by carrying out the necessary investigations alongside identifying lessons that can be learned from incidents that may occur. Band 7s can be highly specialized in their clinical field and are supported to develop specialist skills to provide comprehensive assessment and treatment for patients.

The range of professions under the allied health profession banner is clinically diverse and broad, and therefore the professions attract a wide range of people. However, BAME representation is low. Suzanne Rastrick, Chief AHP Officer for NHS England, highlighted that despite AHPs making up the third largest workforce in the NHS, they have one of the lowest percentages of BAME workers at 12.2 per cent – lower than the UK population average (Rastrick, 2020). This is significantly lower than the NHS workforce average, and when reviewing representation in higher bands (8a and above), this figure drops to less than 10 per cent (Rastrick, 2020).

Case study

Kiran* is an experienced OT, having worked in a variety of trusts. She qualified in 2015 and was the only OT of Indian heritage in her team of ten. Kiran actually wanted to be a physiotherapist, but while completing shadowing experience in a falls clinic, she saw an OT and was intrigued by their job role. She researched the career further and saw the various fields that OTs can work in, including mental health, which was her area of interest. After her student placements, she preferred working in physical health, and she embarked on a career in the NHS, where she wanted to make a difference to others. For Kiran, there is a meaningful reward in helping people of all ages and backgrounds, particularly those who otherwise would not be able to access healthcare due to accessibility or affordability.

After qualifying, Kiran spent a year working in a medium-sized trust, gaining experience in medical elderly care. Here she developed her assessment and discharge planning skills before moving on to work in neurorehabilitation: a clinical specialty working with brain injury and stroke patients. For OTs, this involves supporting cognitive rehabilitation, reintegration to normal life and discharge planning to ensure a safe return to life outside of hospital. It is a challenging but rewarding area that supports people to regain a sense of independence and function after a life-changing event.

As she looks back on when she first became an OT, Kiran says she didn't realize how much responsibility her role of treating patients would entail and the impact it would have on people's lives. As a clinician, she feels she can make a difference, and she is now keen to develop her experience to support wider service improvements. This is one of her reasons for pursuing a research post in health inequalities, where she is keen to improve patient outcomes and experiences for BAME patients.

Whilst she was studying at university, her tutors were friendly, some more than others. All her tutors were white, and in her experience, they were not always culturally aware. For example, at Christmas time, there would be acknowledgement of the festive period and conversations about how people were celebrating, but come Diwali or Eid, there was no mention of this to students who were participating in celebratory events. Ramadan was another example: when Muslim students said that they were observing Ramadan, some tutors would respond positively and engage in a conversation about how they could support students, whereas others would be silent, opting not to say anything. It is puzzling that university lecturers would not want to be curious and ask questions about how their students are marking festive events that are important to them, for example, whether this impacts their studies and whether there is anything that the university could do to support them during this time. But when it comes to Christmas, there can be an expectation to partake in Christmas dinner and secret santa, even if they do not celebrate Christmas ordinarily.

Clinical experiences

AHP students complete a variety of clinical placements to enhance experience and exposure to the clinical environment. Kiran's first placement was in paediatric neurology and the paediatric intensive care unit. After that, she completed a six-week placement in intermediate care, supporting the rehabilitation of people recovering from acute illness. Her next placement was a teenage mental health unit, where she observed stark differences in patient demographics. It was here that most patients with mental health issues were of BAME background, and she felt that this meant she had some common ground with the patients in this setting. Most OTs complete a role-emerging placement: an opportunity for a student to develop an occupational therapy service to support service users. Kiran's was in a sheltered accommodation unit for elderly people, where the majority of the service users were white and elderly. It was here that she felt most out of place.

She was the only BAME person on placement, amongst her team and service users; she describes feeling othered by staff and service users. For example, service users would talk about the First World War and tell Kiran, 'You won't understand this,' which was incorrect: she was born in the UK, and her grandfather took part in the war. There was an assumption that she did not understand British idioms, despite being from the UK. This situation was frustrating, as not only did it question her affiliation with the UK as her home, it also demonstrated a lack of awareness and appreciation for the 1 million soldiers of Indian origin who fought for the UK in the First World War. In Birmingham, where Kiran is from, the representation of Indian people in the war is commemorated with statues and memorials; however, on placement, none of this was acknowledged or even understood, leaving Kiran feeling out of place.

Kiran's final placement was the first where she met other BAME

OTs, nurses and doctors. The service user population was diverse, as the placement was in a large teaching trust. In her first role after she qualified, almost 50 per cent of the team were BAME, which for AHPs is unusual. Despite this, various factors meant there was a clear divide between members of the team. Whilst she doesn't believe that this was entirely because of racism, there were stark differences in how some team members were treated. Cultural awareness in the team was limited, which was made obvious by the lack of willingness of some team members to engage with BAME colleagues. At lunchtime, BAME staff tended to sit in the canteen, whereas the rest of the team would sit in another office. Kiran can't say for certain that this was because of racism, but it is interesting to note that the team would generally split in this way.

Kiran became good friends with her ethnic minority colleagues, because they were able to discuss in a safe space the similar issues that affected them and to feel heard and understood. For example, if she had a racist patient, Kiran felt she could offload the experience with her fellow BAME colleagues but not necessarily to her white colleagues, who didn't understand the impact that such experiences had.

One day, one of Kiran's BAME colleagues had an outburst after months of feeling targeted by microaggressions. Her colleague felt isolated and as though she had to watch herself constantly around the team for fear they would make an issue about something. The colleague was asked to change her working location, and she became incredibly angry about it. Her response was extreme, but it was a build-up of months of being ignored, being reported to managers without any prior conversation taking place, being left out at team socials and meetings, and feeling generally excluded from the wider team.

Kiran was keen to progress in her career and thought that the opportunities at her current workplace were limited. She wanted to experience different clinical areas, which her trust didn't offer. She did not have any conversations with her supervisor regarding her progression, but she was a proactive individual who sought to identify her own opportunities. She did this by networking with others whilst actively searching for job roles, and she successfully landed a role in neurological rehabilitation at another trust. On her first day, she walked into the office and felt the stark fact of being the only BAME person in the room. Everyone stared as she knocked on the door and walked in to introduce herself. She felt a sea of faces looking back at her and recalls feeling as though she stuck out like a sore thumb. It was a massive culture shift from where she had worked previously. She noticed that the informal conversations were different. For example, in her last trust, colleagues would informally talk about TV shows, life events, funny situations they had seen and so forth. At her new place, the conversation was around getting drunk, nights out, who had slept with whom and gossiping. She reports that explicit, unprofessional conversations were the norm, but this was not something she wanted to participate in. These topics were the basis of conversation at lunchtimes, and she found it hard to fit in to such conversations, as she was not interested in this behaviour.

She says that her colleagues were nice and friendly people with whom she got on well but she felt that it was hard to fit in and she experienced a major cultural shock. It took time to find common ground. The team changed as people moved on to their next clinical rotation, and new people came in. This is quite common in AHP professions like physiotherapy and occupational therapy, where colleagues experience 'rotations' in different clinical environments to support clinical experience and development. When the team rotated, she became good friends with new members of the team, one of whom was another BAME AHP. For Kiran, this was someone she could connect and share her identity with.

She was there for around 18 months and always felt well supported by her supervisor. Her supervisor also supported her with looking for other jobs to further her neurology experience. Kiran always had common ground with BAME consultants and describes having good working relationships with them. This meant that she felt more confident to pursue her knowledge and ask questions, because there were people there who looked like her and she felt represented in the wider workplace. Representation is indeed powerful and has an unspoken impact on those who are under-represented.

Having BAME colleagues makes her feel more confident. Knowing that she is a skilled and talented OT, I asked why she thinks that she lacks confidence when BAME colleagues are not present. She replied that she worries about being judged because she looks different. Sometimes there is an attitude that comes with the question, 'Where are you from?', with people assuming that you can't speak English. She hears patients who complain about not understanding international nurses when they are speaking or say that things have not been explained properly, even when they have. Hearing this criticism leads Kiran to feel concerned about patients saying things like that about her, despite her being an articulate and intelligent OT. Having another BAME colleague makes her feel more at ease in situations like this, because if someone does make racist comments, she feels there is someone else who understands how this feels.

Kiran's supervisor always supported her as best she could. Kiran had a difficult time when her grandma became unwell, and her supervisor gave her the time and space she needed to process what was happening without worrying about work. When religious festivals like Diwali would come round, Kiran's supervisor would support her annual leave requests, send her a text message to say happy Diwali and show a genuine interest in how her celebrations had gone. No other colleagues did that, and for Kiran, it meant she felt valued and accepted in the workplace.

Microaggressions

Whilst Kiran's supervisor was fantastic and supportive, the biggest issue she had whilst working at this trust was microaggressions from her manager. The term 'microaggression' was first developed by Chester Pierce in the 1970s (Pierce, 1974) and is widely used today to describe hostile, offensive or discourteous interactions with a tone that reinforces inequitable social norms (Williams, 2020). Microaggressions can prevail in everyday occurrences and in environments where there is a stigma or power imbalance between groups, and they are commonly associated with racism. The term was first introduced to describe the black–white interactions observed by Pierce in his field as a psychiatrist, but today it has expanded to cover various marginalized groups. Whilst the term indicates small or subtle interactions through the term 'micro', their effects can be chilling and impactful. Effects of microaggressions include stress, emotional harm, feelings of embarrassment or intimidation, feeling undermined and feeling exposed or vulnerable (Johnson and Johnson, 2019).

Consistent exposure to microaggressions can have a negative impact on one's mental health and wellbeing (Hollowood, 2022). It can lead to feelings of isolation and exclusion, and it can negatively impact professional self-esteem, having a subsequent effect on professional performance. It can lead to overworking, as one feels the need to prove oneself to maintain the same level of performance at work as the microaggressors. Doing this all the time can take an emotional toll, leading to burnout and poor mental health. Microaggressions are often experienced as an 'everyday' form of racism, where someone may not even be aware they are doing it or experiencing it, as it is context dependent and can therefore be difficult to define. Microaggressions exist in various forms and can be verbal or non-verbal (Gueits, 2022). The three types of microaggressions are defined below.

- **Microinsult**: Rude, insensitive comments that disrespect an individual's race or identity. For example, rudely asking someone, 'Are you from here?'

- **Microassault**: Purposeful words or abuse intended to discriminate against the victim. For example, moving away from someone when they are standing next to you at the bus stop.

- **Microinvalidation**: When someone attempts to ignore, discredit or dismiss the experiences of an individual. For example, not listening to or ignoring your work colleagues.

The presence of microaggressions in healthcare is well documented, with three in five doctors reporting experiences of microaggressions in the NHS (Campbell, 2023). Various NHS educational bodies offer resources on understanding and navigating microaggressions, such as the NHS Leadership Academy's course on how to deal with microaggressions and Health Education England's resources on navigating microaggressions (2024). These are freely available on their websites.

Kiran describes her experiences of microaggressions, which have prevailed throughout her career. Whilst working in neurorehabilitation, her manager would regularly assume that all Asian people spoke the same language. This is as absurd as thinking that every French person can speak German because they share the same skin colour. He failed to recognize the differences in languages like Urdu, Hindi, Punjabi and Arabic, to name a few. Each language is different, and therefore such an assumption demonstrates ignorance.

When a new patient of Asian background would arrive, Kiran would generally know what their cultural background was likely to be. For example, knowing that someone called Aysha Begum is likely to be of Pakistani or Bangladeshi background and therefore speak Urdu or Bengali, or that someone called Balvinder Kaur is likely to be of Indian background and therefore speak Hindi or Punjabi. Someone who is culturally aware of that background is likely to be able to work out such differences before speaking to the person. And someone who perhaps isn't aware of other cultures is likely to not have this background or to make incorrect assumptions. Kiran didn't expect her manager to know the difference, but she did expect him to ask patients and his colleague what languages they spoke.

Instead, Kiran's manager assumed that she spoke the same language as all Asian patients and would therefore allocate said patients to her caseload, even if she didn't speak their language. The first time this happened, she asked her manager what language the patient spoke. Her manager didn't know. This suggests that he made a couple of assumptions: that the Asian patient did not speak English and that Kiran and the patient spoke the same language, even though they didn't. She raised this and he was apologetic. It occurred in a team meeting where others were present, and she felt like she was in the wrong for speaking up to her senior by challenging his assumptions. But she did it anyway because it mattered. She thought that this would be the end of it and brushed it off; however, it happened again.

The second time, she wondered whether she should speak up or not. The previous events played on her mind, so she decided to raise it with her supervisor instead. Her supervisor addressed it with her manager, and agreed that it was not acceptable, but then it happened again. By this time, Kiran was becoming frustrated. It felt like a consistent microaggression, and despite her addressing it twice, his behaviour didn't change. It was further frustrating to her that she had an Asian physiotherapist colleague whose manager never assumed that he could speak the same language as other Asian patients. Her colleague's manager would book an interpreter unless her colleague volunteered to translate when he was able to speak the same language as the patient, whereas any Asian patient would be allocated to Kiran, with the assumption that they both spoke the same language. There was also an expectation that she would translate for patients, even when she already had a full diary for that day.

This continued, and one day she became upset. Her supervisor recognized that this was not okay, and both she and Kiran spoke with the manager. Kiran informed her manager that he had upset her with his consistently incorrect assumptions. Asking the simple question of what language she spoke would have prevented this situation from escalating. Again, he was very apologetic, as though it were happening for the first time. Overall, this scenario demonstrates the impact of microaggressions and a lack of awareness of how assumptions about other people may affect them. A lack of cultural awareness is another issue here, as well as the inability to be curious and ask the right questions, such as: what language do you speak, and should I book an interpreter for this patient? Kiran didn't expect her manager to remember what languages she spoke but she did expect him to ask. This situation contributed to her making the decision to leave. She didn't like feeling as though she stuck out all the time because of her race, and although most of her colleagues were friendly, she wanted to be somewhere where there was a wider mix of people and to expand her neurorehabilitation experience.

She moved to a teaching trust just as the Covid-19 pandemic hit. She had a couple of other BAME colleagues in her team, and there was a mix of people in the wider team. She developed a good working relationship with one of her colleagues, with whom she could offload when they experienced microaggressions or racist incidents at work. Having a colleague who understood how such behaviours made her feel provided a comfort and confidence in the workplace. She reports that most of her colleagues, particularly those of a senior background, i.e., band 6 level, were of white, middle-class background. Her white colleagues came across as not having had much exposure to people of different backgrounds. On the other hand, the support workers tended to be much more aware of multicultural differences and receptive to cultural nuances that staff of different backgrounds might have. She recalls one support worker who would make the effort to understand patients and colleagues, regardless of their cultural background. She would ask Kiran and her colleagues whether they'd had a good Eid or Diwali celebration. If she had patients who were non-English speakers, she would make the effort to learn simple words so she could communicate with them. This small but powerful effort was significant in breaking down barriers and enabling inclusivity. It supported fellow colleagues and patients to feel respected and supported regardless of their background. They felt welcomed and included, which supported better working relationships. Interestingly, most of the support workers (band 3 and band 4) were of BAME background; however, the more senior the role, the less it seemed that diversity and inclusivity principles were considered, despite two band 7 managers being BAME. Seeing people who look like her in managerial positions gave Kiran a sense that she could also achieve such roles, as well as a sense of feeling understood if she did have any cultural issues to report.

The majority of her experiences of discrimination at the teaching trust were microaggressions. For example, one of the senior OTs who was white would tell Kiran every time she made a curry at home. They would both be sitting in the office, and her colleague would say, 'Kiran, I made a daal at the weekend,' or, 'I had a mango lassi yesterday,' or, 'My mum's gone to India.' Kiran's initial response was to be polite; however, as it continued, it left her feeling a strangeness about her colleague, who, Kiran felt, didn't need to tell her every time she did something that was remotely Indian. As we discussed this, Kiran said she didn't think her colleague was being malicious but rather was trying too hard.

On the flipside, when she was having lunch with her colleagues another time, one of them outrightly asked her in an abrupt manner, 'Do you eat curry every day?' At the time, she thought it was a weird thing to ask. She wondered if she was being dramatic or reading too much into it. The two had had no relationship prior to this engagement. They were part of the same wider team, but Kiran did not have much of a relationship with this person. They had never spoken or conversed much either. At the time, Kiran felt embarrassed and laughed it off, but she felt uncomfortable with her colleague questioning her in that manner. If the two had had a friendly relationship, or if her colleague had been inquisitive rather than direct, it would have been different. After Kiran answered that no, she didn't, her colleague then asked her, 'So, were you born in England?' Kiran was mortified. Here she was, with her British accent, being questioned by her white colleague about whether she was 'from' the UK. The incident brought back racist incidents from her childhood in which racial taunts were chanted. This is a true example of a microaggression. Situations like this enhance animosity, as the privileged white person doesn't think twice about how their actions or statements will affect another person and feels entitled enough to be able to ask a question that has an offensive undertone.

Kiran likens the above scenario to a common question that many BAME people face: 'So, where are you from?' The insinuation is that we are not from here, and it almost questions whether we should be here when it's asked in a particular tone (those who know, know). It tends to be a loaded question, and whilst some people are genuinely curious, the person being asked can feel the intention behind that question in the manner in which it is asked. Kiran commonly hears it from patients, some of whom are curious and some of whom are ignorant, but she occasionally hears it from colleagues too.

A patient recently asked her, 'Where are you from?' Kiran told her that she is originally from Birmingham, and the patient scoffed and said, 'No, where are you really from?' Kiran asked her to clarify what she meant, and the patient said, 'No, you know what I mean, where are you really from?' Kiran told her that she is of Indian background – if that was what she was referring to. The patient laughed and said, 'Yeah, thought so. So does your dad wear a turban and that?' Comments like this demonstrate the ignorance that staff face when working with the public. But from an employer's perspective, why does the NHS not provide staff with ways of managing this? Why do we leave staff to deal with these microaggressions on their own? Incidents like this can lower an individual's self-esteem and confidence in their identity, both as an individual and as a professional.

For newly qualified professionals, such incidents can be challenging to deal with. They are trying to find their feet in their new role, build their professional identity and solidify their knowledge. Microaggressions like those detailed above can impact on an individual's professional and personal growth, particularly if their identity or race is under constant observation and questioning from both patients and colleagues alike. Kiran says that with experience and confidence, dealing with such incidents has become easier. But it would have been much easier not to have had to deal with them in the first place.

Another common microaggression Kiran experiences is her white colleagues confusing her with her black female colleague. For example, they might say, 'Oh Kiran, sorry, Andrea*.' Now, this is problematic. The two women do not look alike. Kiran is Indian and Andrea is black. Kiran has a clear English accent, and Andrea has a distinct Scottish accent. They aren't the only two who experience this confusion with names; two of the Indian support workers' names are commonly mixed up by white staff too, and this phenomenon only seems to happen with BAME colleagues.

Dealing with racism

One day, Kiran worked with a patient with dementia who made a racist comment. Kiran informed her manager about the incident, expecting some form of support. Instead, her manager excused the patient's behaviour, as she had a dementia diagnosis. And, of course, the dementia could well have played a part, as the patient may not have had the mental capacity to understand the implications of her comments. But one would expect a manager to at least empathize with Kiran's experience of racist abuse. Her manager's poor response of excusing the racism without asking Kiran if she was okay or validating her experience as one that should not have happened is concerning. The lack of emotional validation after someone has experienced racism as part of the staff experience must be addressed.

Some people can be lenient towards racism that older patients exhibit. But should this be tolerated? Kiran thinks not. And I would agree. There are certain behaviours and words that are unacceptable across the board, whether or not a person has mental capacity. And staff should not be conditioned to accept such behaviour because, 'That's how they used to think in the old days.' There are no excuses for racism. Language is powerful, and to be subjected to racist language without anyone validating how you may feel about experiencing this can be isolating, devaluing and demoralizing.

It is incredibly demoralizing to experience a situation in which someone undermines you and criticizes you unjustly and then not be supported through that experience. From an organizational perspective, it impacts an employee's job satisfaction if they do not feel safe at work. Whilst a racist patient cannot be discharged or removed from the organization if their medical condition poses a risk to life, managers can and should ensure that their staff feel safe, heard, protected and supported as a minimum. One trust has enacted a policy in which staff who are subjected to racist abuse can terminate care, with a letter being sent to the patient to state that such views are not in line with the trust's values and behaviours and therefore they do not wish to see the patient at the trust if this behaviour continues. This represents a powerful stance of protecting staff from discrimination and prejudice. If this policy is implemented as well as enacted, it will likely see a reduction in racism, bullying or harassment from patients and result in a better staff experience.

The importance of language and understanding

Kiran is currently working on a research project about health inequalities. The project reviews engagement in the neurorehabilitation of patients who do not speak English. Working in a regional neurosurgical centre means it is common to have patients from diverse backgrounds. One incident that inspired this research project was an Asian patient who was admitted for neurosurgery. Following his surgery, he was left with deafness in one ear. He was asleep one day, with his deaf ear up and his good ear on the pillow. A nurse entered the room to ask him a question and when he did not respond, the nurse assumed that he could not speak English. This was documented in his clinical records, along with the assumption that the patient spoke Urdu. Kiran went to see the patient, and after seeing in his clinical record that he could not speak English, she booked an interpreter.

The patient followed the interpreter's translations for a short time, and then in clear English said, 'I'm so sorry, I just can't hear you, I'm deaf in this ear.' Kiran was stunned. The patient replied in a Yorkshire accent, 'Yeah, I can speak English. I was born and raised in Yorkshire.' As a professional, she felt embarrassed that her colleague had assumed he couldn't speak English, resulting in an interpreter being booked to communicate with him when there was no need for this. Not only is this a waste of professional resources and the time of the interpreter who was not actually needed, but it also demonstrates an ignorance in communicating with patients of different backgrounds and understanding what language they speak.

She recalls another patient who had been admitted with a subarachnoid haemorrhage. This is a bleed in the brain, and close monitoring for further headaches soon after the event is essential. The patient was of Bengali background and spoke little English. As the nurses completed ward round, it was known that this patient could not speak English well. When she was asked whether she'd had any headaches (in English), the patient smiled. Kiran went to assess this patient and booked an interpreter to support the communication. At the end of the session, the patient complained of a bad headache. Kiran informed the nursing team that the patient was complaining of severe headaches, and the nurses responded that she'd not asked for painkillers or said she'd had a headache when asked. The patient was known to have a language barrier, so one would think that health professionals would use the available resources to reduce the impact of the language barrier (the trust offers a language line service – a 24/7 service that can be accessed via telephone to communicate with the patient in their language, as well as interpreters).

Not using these resources and instead assuming that the patient is fine poses a patient safety risk: their needs are not communicated or understood effectively, despite the resources being available to minimize such risk. This is particularly relevant in conditions like subarachnoid haemorrhage, where the longer it takes to diagnose, the more brain tissue dies, thereby contributing to worse patient outcomes. A simple resolution would be to use the translation tools available or ask interpreters about the basic words needed to be able to communicate yes/no questions effectively with patients.

Kiran feels strongly that she will always be an advocate for patients who cannot speak English, remembering her own experiences of her grandparents having limited English and the difficulties they had in accessing healthcare. She feels exasperated by how often no one calls an interpreter for patients who cannot speak English. She regularly requests interpreters but feels conscious that, despite it being important for patient safety and the patient experience, colleagues might think she is 'nagging' about this issue because she is always the one advocating for it.

In Kiran's experience, issues within the NHS around race are systematic. For example, if you make a mistake in the workplace and you are Asian, you are viewed very differently to (and more negatively than) a white person making the same mistake. On one of the wards Kiran works on, some nurses are of international background. Kiran has noticed that when they make a mistake, it is managed much more formally than when a white colleague makes a mistake: the mistakes of her colleagues who have an international background are addressed with a closed, personal conversation behind closed doors, whereas the mistakes of her white colleagues are addressed informally with a laid-back approach and not spoken of again. Such differences can impact how someone progresses in their career: while the nurses who have an international background are formally reprimanded, their white colleagues are supported when they make mistakes and still have the confidence to continue. This can affect someone's confidence in their own abilities as a healthcare professional, especially if they feel unsupported and victimized for making the same mistakes as their white colleagues and observe that these colleagues do not receive the same formal reprimand.

Representation
Representation of people from BAME backgrounds among staff supports trust-building with patients, as they are able to relate to someone who can understand their background, culture and, sometimes, language. Kiran emphasizes that the NHS needs to be better at improving representation of people from different communities, because the UK is not a monoracial society. On our streets, we see people of different backgrounds, cultures and ethnicities, but if this is not represented in something like healthcare, then how is that healthcare truly representative? Kiran was surprised to learn that 25 per cent of the NHS is BAME, making it the largest BAME employer in Europe. Compared with the overall UK population, where BAME people make up 15 per cent of the population, the NHS technically has an over-representation. However, it is important to understand the context: the majority of those people are in lower banded roles, where racism tends to be more overt and direct. As colleagues ascend through the hierarchy, the racism becomes more covert, for example:

being held to a far higher standard than your peers; subtle comments; feeling like you must work twice as hard to get half as far. It makes you consider why you work in the NHS if this is how you are made to feel. And it reminds me of the importance of values and of having your own set of values that dictates why you do what you do. That way, when challenges do arise – which can happen in any situation – you can remind yourself what you are doing it for.

When considering whether she is treated with respect, inclusion and equity in the workplace, Kiran says she thinks she is not treated differently to anyone else – no better and no worse. She thinks this is because she has built a reputation of being good at what she does, despite her experiences of regular microaggressions. She has excellent clinical skills and is known for this. However, when asked whether she has had to work harder than her peers to be treated in the same way, she says yes. For example, she was working a split post to support two services. Whilst managing two services, she was also expected to deliver a neuro-oncology service development project, alongside running as an extra member of staff in acute or outpatient clinics when there was a higher demand. She felt exhausted from doing three different roles but thought this was not understood, recognized or appreciated. She was also having a difficult time personally – her father was unwell and she was responsible for taking him to his medical appointments. Yet, during this time, no one checked in with her to ask how she was managing and if she needed any further support. In comparison, her other colleagues of the same level were working in one service. Her manager was aware of the challenges experienced with low staffing and high demand, but this was not acknowledged consistently during the challenging period. At the end, though, her efforts were recognized, which, whilst appreciated, came a little later than it should have done.

We spoke about the importance of representation. Having BAME colleagues who were in senior roles but also demonstrated the courage to speak up and challenge racial inequalities gave her the confidence to deal with the racial challenges of the NHS. The NHS increasingly relies on international nurses, some of whom are not confident enough to speak up. This means that others don't speak up, and a culture develops where everyone is fearful to speak up. Not only does it become harder to challenge racism the longer it goes on, but it also ends up leading to people internalising discriminatory comments, whcih can become emotionally difficult to manage.

Representation is no doubt important, and we often see it 'celebrated' in months like South Asian Heritage Month (SAHM), Black History Month, etc. Just recently, Kiran feels critical of the opinion that the best way to demonstrate inclusivity is through eating different cultural foods. The issue is that when diversity is celebrated as eating different foods and admiring cultural dress, everyone wants to join in. However, when it comes to providing equity in the same space, respecting cultures and providing a space to validate our thoughts and feelings, this becomes too uncomfortable to speak about or carry out. During SAHM, her colleagues (who have never discussed what racism may look like in their team or workplace) decided to have a 'fuddle', bringing in different South Asian foods. Kiran brought some traditional food that was slightly different from the Sainsbury's samosas that the others had brought in. She shared sweets from her home after a traditional Sikh festival, but staff were reluctant to try them, sticking their noses up and turning their faces away.

The issue that Kiran takes with such events is that, in some spaces, diversity is presented in the way that others wish to see it, not how it truly is. These spaces want diversity to fit their narrative – for you to be the way they wish to see you and accept that – instead of seeing who you truly are and what you bring. She spoke of the irony that such events end up with BAME people sitting in one group to engage with each other whilst their white colleagues sit together somewhere else. It brings out a difference even though it's meant to bring people together. Whilst there is some truth in the sentiment that it brings people together by providing an opportunity to share cultures and break down barriers, it can feel like a tick-box exercise. Everyone has a bit of nice food and some cultural music, but very little actually changes to enable true inclusion and respect of diversity. It can make you feel like a show horse – being told to demonstrate your culture when someone wants you to through events they decide to showcase. But when it comes to addressing racism and the lack of representation in senior posts, this is ignored or not discussed.

Despite her experiences, Kiran still thinks that the trust where she works now is the most inclusive one she's worked for, even though she still experiences racism there too. It is a trust where she has met many colleagues from diverse backgrounds and made friends with people who share similarities, and therefore it is a place where she feels represented and able to form connections with people. As we ended the discussion, I asked Kiran what advice she would give to her younger self entering the NHS. She said it was: be more confident in speaking up, and don't be scared to speak up for yourself if someone says something to you. Sometimes, after a situation, Kiran thinks she hasn't responded well in the moment. After having some time to reflect, she considers the situation and goes back to respond to it appropriately. Dana James-Edwards in her blog for The King's Fund (2022) also provides useful advice on deciding how to respond to microaggressions, including considering:

- whether you feel resilient enough to engage
- whether you are able to respond without being unprofessional yourself
- how the individual may respond to your reply
- whether the environment and situation is appropriate
- how best to express yourself in such a situation.

However you choose to respond, don't feel bad if it doesn't go how you'd hoped. Equally, don't think that you are the only one who should be challenging microaggressions, as everyone has a responsibility to call out such behaviour when it takes place.

Don't be afraid to share your experiences, because when you do, it validates how you feel about such injustice. Sometimes you find other people to share the experience with who have experienced similar situations, and you realize you are not alone. Whenever she talks about BAME experiences or language barriers in her team, Kiran feels she is 'annoying' people by bringing it up. But not consistently addressing the issues means they don't change. It can be hard, and confidence comes with time and experience, but it also comes from knowing who you are and what you bring. As vital a role as your occupation in life is, it does not define you as a person. Remember that. Work on ways to find out who you are, what you stand for and what you will speak up about when you need to. Sometimes we can be one-dimensional and focus only on our careers or the roles that we play, and we forget that we are people behind the job roles too. It could be that you feel you have lost a part of yourself in the process of getting to where you are, because you have sacrificed so much time and effort, but this is when it's even more important to know what you stand for.

The People, Environment, Occupation (PEO) model in occupational therapy analyses this, arguing that the workplace is a huge part of one's identity (Law *et al.*, 1996). Often we introduce ourselves using our job role because what we do is a part of who we are. Your work takes up most of your time, particularly if you work full time (or more), and it's the environment in which you spend most of your day. If it is not an equitable space, it isn't inclusive, and if you feel like you don't belong there, then that becomes an issue.

Kiran previously studied sociology, and so we discussed the identities one holds in life. Kiran describes how you hold two identities for your cultural identity: your identity at home and the one you present in your workspace. You can't be your full Asian self at work, so you must water it down when you are there. And when you are at home, you can't be your full white self. She thinks that she is not the same at work as she is at home. En route to work she blasts out her Punjabi music, but when she pulls up at work, she turns it off, as she feels it's not recognized as part of that culture or identity. One could argue that the workplace requires a professional identity and ask whether it is a place to start blasting out Punjabi music. Alternatively, one could ask whether it is an appropriate place for colleagues to be discussing how drunk they got at the weekend or who slept with whom; but still, that seems to be culturally acceptable. While discussing this, Kiran speaks admirably about her BAME colleague who sings Indian songs without any apology at work. He may come across as eccentric to some, but it is an identity he is proud to exhibit in the workplace and he does so with confidence. But you can become conditioned when you are the only one in the team – feeling like you are the odd one out – so then you find ways of hiding your identity to almost 'fit in' with the others, even though you don't feel that this is what makes you 'you'. So be you, and don't be afraid to showcase your identity in the workplace.

Reflective questions

* Have you experienced microaggressions at work or in education? Write about the experience. What happened, how did it make you feel, what did you take away from it, and what would you do if it happened again?

* Have you seen a colleague be impacted by racism? How did you support them? If you have experienced it personally, was it handled appropriately? If not, what can you do about it?

* If you are a manager, consider what practices you have within your team or department that support BAME staff if they experience racism. Reflect on whether they are validated and supported during the situation.

* Does your organization have a policy on how to manage racism? Is the policy effective? Was it co-created with BAME individuals, and is it fit for purpose?

* How will you respond to microaggressions that you are aware of? Is there anyone who could help you, or are there resources that would support your development in this area? Have you seen other colleagues being affected by microaggressions, and might you be able to reach out and support them?

— CHAPTER 4 —

Case Study 2: A Nurse's Journey

This chapter will discuss:

- the journey of a BAME nurse
- BAME representation in nursing
- discrimination and how Alisha* overcame this.

This case study highlights a nurse's journey – from joining the NHS as a healthcare assistant to becoming a nurse. Nursing is by far one of the most challenging professions for many reasons. There is currently a worldwide shortage of nurses, and in the UK, we are seeing an exodus of skilled, compassionate nurses from the profession, citing reasons such as 'poor pay', 'burnout' and feeling overworked and understaffed (Argyrides *et al.*, 2023). The responsibility of the role is significant, and particularly post pandemic, nurses – as well as most colleagues I have worked with – say that they have more responsibilities than they are paid for and that they feel underappreciated.

BAME representation in nursing

In the NHS, people are often referred to by their band, which denotes their level in the hierarchy that governs the NHS. The 'highest' band before VSM or director level is band 9, and the 'lowest' is band 1. Most nurses of BAME background tend to be employed at band 5, which is entry level for a qualified nurse. During my time in the NHS, I have spoken to many who have trained for several years yet remain at junior level. I recall a conversation with a nursing colleague, Aisha, who qualified at the same time as me. I progressed into a senior role after a couple of years and then moved into management, whereas Aisha remained in the same post. I asked her why she had not pursued progression in her career despite being a capable nurse, and she responded with the phrase 'nursing nepotism'. Unfortunately, being promoted based on whom rather than what you know is widespread in nursing. This prevents BAME people from progressing, as often they are not part of the clique that decides on such promotions (Kahin and Khan, 2023).

Historically, BAME nurses have been significantly over-represented in lower bands. In 2014, there were no BAME nurses at band 8 level, and the BAME workforce was so significantly under-represented that black staff were three times less likely than white staff to be in band 8a roles and above (Sprinks, 2014). BAME staff accounted for more than 40 per cent of cases being referred to the Nursing and Midwifery Council (Launder, 2020), and it is likely that they were referred after staff faced disciplinary action from their trusts. In seven trusts at the time of Kline's report in 2014, more than 50 per cent of disciplinary cases in the trusts reviewed were against BAME staff. Furthermore, NHS Leadership Academy data shows that a nursing leadership course implemented in 2013 had 315 recruits, of whom only 4 per cent were from a non-white background; to attend the course, employees required their employer's approval (Calkin, 2013).

BAME representation in nursing remains low, despite steps being taken to improve this. The Royal College of Nursing (RCN) runs targeted leadership programmes, and I was invited to speak to a cohort of 30 band 5 nursing colleagues on one of these programmes. A year later, some participants reported progressing into band 6 roles, and some were soon to commence senior roles following the programme. However, a high attrition rate remains in nursing, particularly amongst newly qualified and student nurses, with one in nine nurses leaving the profession (Palmer and Rolewicz, 2022).

Alisha's journey into healthcare

For this case study, I interviewed Alisha. Alisha is a young, determined nurse who, after completing her A levels, decided to enter the NHS as a healthcare assistant. She worked in operating theatres, and whilst it took some time to understand the complexities of her new role, she enjoyed it. However, there was one issue with this role – wearing the hijab. She had worn the hijab – a headscarf worn by some Muslim women as part of their faith – for her whole life. When she started working, she was told that she could not wear her hijab in theatre. This was due to infection control restrictions stating that outside clothing, which could pose an infection risk, could not be worn in theatre because it is a sterile environment. She contacted the infection control department to get advice on what she could do. She had various Muslim colleagues who were already complying with this rule, but she did not feel comfortable doing so. Whilst infection control is a top priority in healthcare, there was no attempt to support inclusivity by considering how she could be supported to wear a form of hijab in theatre. Alisha decided to purchase a separate garment specifically to wear in theatre so that she could feel comfortable in the workplace. This request was declined, and she thought that she was being made to feel like she was being difficult. From her perspective, she wasn't trying to be difficult – she wanted to feel comfortable in the workplace. Eventually, after working with infection control and ensuring adherence to trust procedures, she was given permission to wear a hijab in theatre. She built relationships with the laundry service staff who washed the hospital clothing, and they were happy to support her in ensuring that the hijab garments were washed as per hospital uniform policy.

Alisha reports that after this, everything she did at work was criticized. For example, if she set up the theatre kit – following the checklist exactly – staff would criticize her and say that it could have been done better, despite it being set up exactly as the protocol dictated. She was compared with other healthcare assistants and criticized if she did not know something that she had no prior experience of. She was not given training on how to respond to or recognize surgical queries but instead was asked to answer the phone and respond to surgical questions from the team, despite not understanding the terminology because she had limited experience in her new role.

After Alisha started wearing the theatre hijab, she noticed that other Muslim colleagues started to wear a theatre-style hijab too. She felt proud that she had been able to instigate a positive change that supported people to feel comfortable at work without compromising on her own values or those of infection control and patient safety. She reflects that this is where she learned to stand her ground – informing colleagues that she would not tolerate poor behaviour when she was spoken to rudely or abruptly. When she first joined the team, her colleagues said that she couldn't do anything right, but the same colleagues lamented losing a valuable team member when she left.

The second issue she had in this role was around awareness of how she practised her faith. Alisha is a devout Muslim, praying five times daily. Her colleagues were baffled by her wanting time to pray during the day, which took 20 minutes at most. At times it could be challenging; however, what made it easier was that her team were accommodating of her need to pray. Other colleagues were condescending, asking, 'How long does it take just to say hi to Allah?' Such a statement, which is Islamophobic, reflects the ignorance that can prevail, even in a professional environment. Alisha now works in private healthcare, where her colleagues are respectful and provide her with the space and time to be able to complete her prayers. Her current colleagues are more attuned, and she thinks that environment and culture make a big difference to her morale, confidence and motivation in her role.

From healthcare assistant to nursing

Whilst working as a healthcare assistant, Alisha decided to apply for nursing training. Initially, her manager said that they were short-staffed and was reluctant to support Alisha's nursing training; however, Alisha was determined to further her own development. Alisha told her manager that she would be applying for nursing whether they were short-staffed or not, and she continued with the programme. She felt upset at not being supported by her manager to complete her nursing training but proud that she had stood up for herself. Being able to stand her ground has helped Alisha to progress in her career, empowering her to advocate for herself, her colleagues and her patients.

She enjoyed studying as a student nurse, but when she commenced clinical placements, she experienced challenges from colleagues who treated students of ethnic minority background differently. Alisha recalls ethnic minority students being singled out for being late and criticized for tasks that they completed. One day, Alisha asked if she could have a space to pray at work, and this request was declined for no clear reason. She describes being constantly monitored by colleagues who did not let her out of their sight on the ward. One day, Alisha and the patient she was working with started to have a conversation. In this conversation, the patient asked her why she seemed anxious. Alisha informed her that she was not permitted to pray but did not want to miss her prayer. The patient asked her to pray in her room whilst she kept watch, which surprised Alisha. With time running out, she quickly agreed. Whilst this may not seem like the most appropriate thing for Alisha to have done, it was more inappropriate that she was failed by not being provided with a prayer space, with no clear reason, forcing her to be in this situation. It is also worth pointing out that such prohibition of practising one's faith contravenes the Equality Act 2010. In healthcare, some patients are more memorable than others and touch your heart in ways you wouldn't expect. This was a particularly tough day and Alisha was feeling low, so she will never forget that patient's kindness – which outweighed that of her employers.

Alisha was excited when she was approaching being newly qualified, but she recognized that the first six months would be a steep learning curve. She reports that there was a 'bitchy' culture in nursing but she had a strong family network who supported her. Her family encouraged her to keep pushing through the challenges she faced early on, giving her the courage to be confident when addressing such issues. She had to move around regularly to support staffing requirements as a new nurse, which was tough. Despite this impacting nurses' morale, confidence and skill, patient care demands mean it is common for nurses to have to move around in this way.

Becoming a nurse

One of Alisha's first roles was in A&E, where she enjoyed the fast-paced and varied work. She recalls a patient in A&E whom she will never forget – a man who came in with a five-day history of constipation. He was reviewed by the medical team with no significant findings, and therefore he was given laxatives and discharged home. A week later, he returned with the same issue. He was rescanned and there was no change, so again he was sent home with laxatives. The following week, the man was readmitted. Alisha recognized him from his previous visits and thought that further investigation was needed. She explained the situation to her manager and wanted her manager to escalate the case to the surgeon (she thought that as a junior nurse, the surgeon may not listen to her). Alisha's manager agreed with her decision to escalate the case but encouraged her to take responsibility and speak to the surgeon directly to highlight her concerns. She did this to support Alisha's personal and professional growth in challenging opinions from senior colleagues. Alisha felt that this was out of her comfort zone and assumed that her manager was asking her to do it because of 'racism', which wasn't the case in this instance. As she reflects on this, she realizes that it was an opportunity for growth, which became a turning point in her career. This situation highlights that difficult situations arise sometimes and that we must address them as best as we can to support our own development. Sometimes we face uncomfortable situations, and others don't always put us in such positions because they want us to struggle; it could be because it helps us to grow.

She went back to the surgeon and explained that she was not willing to discharge the patient. The surgeon asked why, and she explained that the patient had come in three times in three weeks and that his symptoms remained unchanged. Inside, she was terrified, but she remained cool and calm on the surface. The surgeon agreed, went away and completed a colonoscopy. The surgical team then decided to proceed with a laparoscopy. Alisha had used the SBAR acronym (situation; background; assessment; recommendation) to articulate her case. She further decided to take this experience as an opportunity to learn from her medical colleagues, so that in the future, if such a case was to happen again, she would know what to do.

The laparoscopy identified that the patient had a serious condition, bowel ischaemia, where part of his bowel tissue had died. A few weeks later, she saw the patient on another ward she was working on, and he said to her, 'You saved my life.' The patient was a man in his 30s with young kids, and he was grateful to Alisha for her intervention. This scenario taught her that a good manager is one who provides opportunities for you to learn. They stand behind you whilst allowing you the space to take the lead, providing what is needed to fulfil the role. Her manager would always allow Alisha to use her office for prayers when it was available. Being able to fulfil a task that was important for her wellbeing led to her feeling respected and valued in the workplace.

Nursing demands a strong sense of overall responsibility for a patient's care. There are so many professionals who could be involved in a patient's care, and nurses tend to coordinate this and ensure that the patient is seen by these professionals to support their care. For example, a stroke patient may have: a surgeon to complete their surgery; a physiotherapist reviewing their mobility; an OT to support their cognition needs and discharge planning from hospital; a speech and language therapist to help with their speech and swallowing issues; healthcare assistants who support with taking observations and providing care; a psychologist who supports with managing their emotions; a psychiatrist who may provide support if mental health intervention is needed; an orthotist who provides splints and aids to support recovery. These are just some of the healthcare professionals who could be involved, and a nurse oversees this, as well as fulfilling their own duties, which include providing medications and treatments, escalating care when necessary and supporting the patient through their illness. As a nurse, Alisha describes being given the opportunity to develop her skills and access training, but as she progressed, she realized the importance of building strong relationships too. She always prioritized building relationships with at least one pharmacist, a senior nurse and a surgeon so she had access to knowledge from colleagues, benefitting her practice and her patients.

Alisha had a good working relationship with her manager, and she invited her manager to her wedding when she later got married. She felt part of the team and was always provided with space to pray and supported during Ramadan, the month of fasting, and her need for time off at Eid was accommodated. Clinically, she was supported to gain experience in completing male and female catheters, IV fluids administration and managing serious conditions. As she progressed, Alisha gained confidence in articulating how to ask for help or support in the clinical environment. For example, she would do what she could and then review the response. If it did not work and required escalation, she would contact the doctors to say what she had done and then seek advice on what could be done next.

Pushing out of her comfort zone

Alisha is a surgical nurse with passion, but when she moved city, she decided to challenge herself and work in a medical rotational role to experience different medical settings. Alisha was used to the fast-paced nature of surgical nursing, but she found that there was a slower pace in medicals, due to the nature of illnesses experienced in this setting.

There was a big adjustment period when she moved, both personally and professionally, as she settled into her new home and her new job. Her team were supportive and her colleagues were clinically knowledgeable, so Alisha felt like she could learn from them. Whilst her manager was not so confident in her clinical knowledge, she led the team effectively to ensure that safe clinical care was provided in the unit. There can be an assumption that managers are also skilled clinically, but this is not always the case. A managerial skillset differs from a clinical skillset, and the assumption that the manager must know everything is incorrect. Sometimes a great manager is also an excellent clinician, but this is not always the case. Alisha enjoyed working here but she recognized that there was a cliquey environment at times. In nursing, this seems common.

We discussed the nepotism in nursing. She spoke about a colleague who had progressed to ward manager, who despite being a good manager, was not flexible with the requirements of staff. As Alisha became a senior nurse herself, she recognized the importance of being flexible with staff and the benefit this brings. If you know your staff, you know where to give. As a senior nurse, she is more understanding of the challenges that managers face when balancing expectations. She has developed better ways of communicating with senior managers and directors, which she previously did not feel confident doing. This confidence developed after she stopped having access to a prayer space at work and knew she wanted to change this. She spoke to her seniors, who said that they would need to speak to the matron. There was no reason why Alisha couldn't address the issue with the matron herself, so she introduced herself to the matron and explained about not having a prayer space. The matron was accommodating and supported her to find a suitable space.

The hierarchy is real in the NHS, and Alisha had never spoken to a matron before this situation. One of the differences between working in private healthcare and the NHS is that the hierarchy looks very different. In private healthcare, Alisha has a good working relationship with her matron, and they have even shared a lunch break together. She reports that such a thing would never happen in the NHS and that senior staff generally do not mix with junior staff.

One night during the Covid-19 pandemic was very difficult for Alisha. She had a deteriorating patient at work and was having a tough time personally, as her marriage had broken down. She was the most senior person on shift and was therefore responsible for supporting her junior colleagues. She tried to put her personal situation aside and focus on her work. She had a patient who was nearing the end of life, and the junior doctor did not feel confident to sign the patient off. The skill mix was challenging, and the bed manager was requesting to change the ward so that a previous 'red' Covid-19 area could be turned to 'green' so that non-Covid-19 patients could be admitted. The team did not have the right staff to change the ward around and so Alisha declined her request. The bed manager came onto the ward and told Alisha that she could not refuse this change. Alisha informed her that there were two A&E nurses who were about to walk out, and she threatened to leave the shift too. She got her coat on, got her bag and prepared to leave. The bed manager asked her what it would take for her to stay, knowing that the staffing situation was dire. Alisha said that she would not be changing any patients around and wanted to finish her shift without being asked to take on extra patients when the staffing levels and skill mix were already inadequate.

The above scenario is a very tough one. On the one hand, when patients are arriving in A&E and there is nowhere to admit them, it creates a backlog in the department. Equally, when there are not enough staff members on the ward or there is not the correct skill mix to ensure a safe clinical environment in which to care for patients, this increases the risk to patient safety, damages staff morale and exacerbates stress faced by staff. By the end of the shift, Alisha had calmed down, the bed manager returned to the ward and both apologized. Neither person was right or wrong. Both were acting in the best interests of their patients and what they were responsible for. It was a highly intense moment where both could have worked together to find a solution. The two spoke openly and honestly, which led to an increase in respect between them, thereby supporting a better working relationship.

After the shift, because of Alisha's personal issues around her marriage and the intensity of the shift, she went to see her line manager and broke down. Her manager sent her home and told her to take some time to recover. Her manager changed Alisha's next few working shifts to support her, and after these shifts she left this role to move back home.

Alisha took some time to recover and later joined the NHS bank[1] to retain her clinical skills. She enjoyed this part-time role, which helped her to have an occupation and do something familiar. She already had the experience needed for the role, and after six months, she decided that she wanted to return to full-time work.

Whilst looking for a new job, she came across the role in a private hospital. She hadn't expected this, but she wanted a new challenge as she emerged from her divorce and decided to give it a try. She has now been working in the private hospital for two years and is enjoying it. The biggest struggle she had at first was adapting to a slower pace of work. She is used to a fast-paced environment, having worked in the NHS. Her patients in the private hospital are healthy, well and coming in for elective surgery. She has found herself deskilling because cannulas, bloods and nasogastric tubes (where nutrition is provided through a tube through the nose, usually when someone is unable to eat or drink) are not required. Factors that make this a rewarding role for Alisha include higher pay and having the space and time to be able to pray, which are both important factors for her.

The importance of having the right mindset

What comes across when talking to Alisha is that she is a go-getter. Her mindset is what propels her success. Barriers have been in her

---

[1] The NHS bank is a service that provides flexible workforce to the NHS when it is required. Often professionals may choose to do this to support the NHS when there is no staff available for shifts.

way, but she has learned to overcome these and gained confidence in the process. She describes the rejection of not getting roles as being hard initially but has learned that rejection is redirection. She has also learned that, despite being a go-getter, accepting when something doesn't work out as you'd expected is also important. When things don't go as expected, she shifts her mindset and works towards something better. It is easy to become disillusioned because of the race inequality in the NHS, but it is so important to build networks, find people to connect and share your experiences with and know what you want to achieve and work towards it. Alisha says that she has experienced racism with staff and managers who have treated her differently to other colleagues; however, she voices her issue with being treated like this, which has worked well.

When it comes to experiencing racism from patients, Alisha has the clinical experience behind her and the confidence to know she is good at her job. She says that whilst it isn't something she should be experiencing, it doesn't particularly bother her personally. When her junior colleagues experience racism, she gives them the confidence to challenge it. Coming from the NHS, when a mistake is pointed out to Alisha, she asks herself, 'Is it because I'm brown or because I'm wearing hijab?' She observes how her peers are treated to see if there is a difference. If there is, she addresses it, and if there isn't, she accepts it for what it is. Sometimes Alisha feels she needs to challenge her own assumptions; for example, she may assume that a patient is being aggressive because they are racist, when sometimes it is because they are feeling distressed due to pain. Her sense of self-awareness and reflection means she will challenge her own assumptions and has the confidence to raise her opinion where necessary. She isn't afraid to have difficult conversations and doesn't shy away from it.

Alisha's story of working in the NHS and moving to the private sector is an atypical one. Whilst every individual's experiences will be different, it is important to appreciate different perspectives and experiences, and what we can learn from each story. In this case study, themes such as confidence to raise issues, seek different opportunities and take yourself out of your comfort zone have been explored, and I hope you can take this away to apply it in your own situation. The following reflective questions should provide some help with this.

Reflective questions

* If you are looking to progress, have you discussed how you can do this with your line manager or a trusted colleague?

* Review your current job description and the description of the next job you are interested in. If you can provide examples of most of the responsibilities/items on the person specification, consider applying for the role.

* What are your current limiting factors that are stopping you from getting to where you want to be? How can you overcome these?

* Have you created a career map/list of goals? If not, create one to reflect on where you are currently and how you think you could move to the next stage. Identify individuals who may be able to help you with this.

* How will you respond to the challenges that you are currently aware of? Is there anyone who could help you or resources that would support your development in this area?

— CHAPTER 5 —

Case Study 3: From Chaplain to EDI Lead

This chapter will discuss:

- the role of chaplaincy in the NHS
- the importance of values supporting EDI
- what it takes to set up a network
- the challenges of working in EDI.

This case study follows the career journey of Samuel, who went from working in chaplaincy to being EDI lead. The NHS is a vast employer, providing opportunities to work in clinical or non-clinical settings. The scale of the non-clinical setting is sometimes underestimated, but it forms a large proportion of the NHS; without it, the NHS would struggle to function. It includes corporate, IT, estates, pastoral care, cleaning, catering and so much more. Samuel's transition from chaplain to EDI professional is unusual and demonstrates his passion for justice and tackling inequalities.

What is chaplaincy?

Pastoral care, specifically chaplaincy, plays an important role in supporting patients through difficult times. Historically, it was associated with people who have a faith or religion; however, it is open to all people – of faith and no faith. As a healthcare professional, it never really occurred to me that patients who may require pastoral care or faith support would benefit from seeing a chaplain.

However, during the Covid-19 pandemic, the value of chaplaincy was obvious, as so many people sought the support of spiritual guidance and mindfulness during challenging times.

All NHS trusts have a dedicated team of chaplains who support patients and staff. It is a service of spirituality and pastoral care, often underused and under-recognized, that resiliently deals with challenging circumstances involving birth, death, loss and grief on a regular basis. Chaplaincy supports patients (and staff) by empathetically providing support for people so they feel valued, respected and understood as holistic individuals. This can sometimes get lost in the clinical setting, which focuses on diagnosis, treatment and discharge from acute settings.

Samuel's career began in community development in Botswana in a varied role including community development, training and humanitarian aid. It involved supporting people who lived on the peripheries of life and marginalized communities, and these were some of the groups he supported in his health inequalities role too. After taking some time out to travel, he was offered an opportunity to work in the UK to support the development of diverse churches through a one-year programme, after which he successfully attained a chaplaincy role in the NHS.

In his first NHS role, one of Samuel's senior colleagues told him that Africans are lazy and uneducated. Samuel himself is black African and responded by informing his colleague that research shows that African youth are high performers and believe in a strong work ethic (Dago and Ray, 2014). He challenged his colleague and asked him what he really meant by his statement. His colleague claimed that it was a known fact, despite it being a negative stereotype. Samuel informed his senior manager of the conversation, who investigated and decided that discriminatory language had been used. His senior manager offered to mediate but Samuel felt deterred from putting in a formal complaint, as it would be 'my word against his'. Samuel felt that the depth of the offensive comments and their impact was not understood, but he knew that if he claimed that his colleague had said these things and then denied it, it would bring little change. This situation led to Samuel deciding to leave and seeking employment elsewhere.

Situations like the above are rather common. Racism occurs, it's raised as a complaint, the person's experience is not validated and they are told, 'It's your word against theirs.' Victims are dissuaded from making formal complaints because they could be disputed. This places a burden on the marginalized of not only having to experience the difficulty of racism and defend themselves from it, but also experiencing the invalidity of not having their identity respected or valued in the workplace. It is worse if the accusation is about a manager. In some settings, the manager assumes a certain level of 'untouchableness' and the other person is made to feel 'lower' or less valued. The hierarchy of the NHS can deny an equal values base regardless of one's position of power and authority in the system. It is a poor assumption that the manager is more mature than a clinician rather than them being two people who have chosen different career paths. For example, a practitioner may not want to deal with writing business papers and prefer working with patients clinically, but it doesn't necessarily mean that they are less able or mature than the manager, despite the manager being in a higher band, which dictates more pay and responsibility. Unfortunately, banding in the NHS matters, as it is often what the hierarchy is based on, rewarding seniority over values and behaviours in the workplace.

Existing inequalities and the structure of the NHS

Whilst the NHS is changing to emphasize the importance of respect and values, it remains highly process oriented. When engaging with communities, the NHS can be guilty of wanting them to align to its structures rather than doing what works for them. We design it... it must be this way...then we invite you to come to our services. You may have issues that our service can't fix, but we can't always deal with them so we do what we can based on what we think we know. This makes things happen quicker and faster, but it can lead to health inequalities when communities are not heard or their needs are not understood. Some of this is due to the funding model, which rewards hitting targets and achieving goals but fails to consider the experience of people in the system. It desensitizes the experience of patients, reducing people to body parts and illness and failing to account for a holistic view of individuals. Some of the patients' values and ideals are bigger than what needs treating, so how do you honour the entirety of a person whilst maintaining their dignity through treatment?

Having recently worked on a cancer strategy with the local authority, Samuel reflects on the reading age across his city of work. The average reading age of his city is eight years old, but Samuel questions whether the trust's literature reflects that. How do we ensure that the audience understands the information being disseminated? This principle also applies to colleagues across NHS organizations. Is the language used in disciplinary letters appropriate for the people we are writing to? How do we write letters to the public, some of whom may not speak good English? If the community does not have a certain standard of literacy, whether it's because of education, language or the inability to read, how are they accessing services at the same time and same pace as their counterparts who do understand? If they do understand the patient information leaflets, are they able to navigate the complex system effectively?

This complex system consists of independent entities that were developed to meet the health needs of populations. Primary care, secondary care and social care all operate independently and use separate systems for IT, policy management and so forth. This contributes to making the healthcare system a challenging place to navigate, although efforts are being made to bring this together through place-based working. Samuel asks whether we are working for ourselves or for the people. Sometimes in the NHS we review where the funding is coming from and whether we are meeting funding objectives rather than reviewing what is best for the patient and whether we are offering that.

The Covid-19 pandemic revealed the prevalence of myths that exist in the community and impact access to healthcare. Do communities trust that they have a space in clinical services that would do what is best for them? In higher ethnic minority areas across the country, people were afraid to bring their loved ones to hospital. It is therefore likely that some of the disproportionate impact of Covid-19 on ethnic minorities was because people were fearful about bringing their relatives in to seek treatment. This was reflected across various cities where BAME populations exist, such as London, Manchester, Leeds and Bradford, suggesting a lack of trust in services. We also see that people with mental health issues in Gypsy/Roma communities tend to access healthcare later, which can lead to poorer health outcomes. Organizations need to do much more to ensure equity amongst all communities, particularly marginalized ones. The NHS has a corporate responsibility to work for the good of the patients rather than what best suits the organization. It also has a social responsibility that is clearly outlined in its constitution, but how seriously does it take these responsibilities?

An effective system that works for the good of the individual requires humility and consideration of what is best for the person involved. This promotes a willingness to learn from other trusts instead of seeing them as competition. Previously, trusts operated in a competitive manner instead of sharing good practice, but this is now changing with initiatives like GIRFT (Getting It Right First Time), national practice guidelines and regional specialist centres to which smaller trusts can refer patients for specialist input.

Advocating for race equality as a chaplain

Samuel has always had a passion for both chaplaincy and race equality. His MA research was on stress management for staff in an acute setting. This reviewed stress management, psychological first aid, leadership planning and supporting teams in transition, all of which supported him in his role of managing Race Equality Networks (RENs).

Equity and EDI were two key important issues to resolve for Samuel as a chaplain. A key priority early on in his chaplaincy role was to address a pressing issue of managing the deaths of patients from Muslim communities. The trust was in an area that had a high Muslim population, but there were multiple complaints about deaths not being handled in line with the practices that mattered to the Muslim community. Samuel contacted Muslim funeral directors to ask how the trust could better approach the death of Muslim patients. He felt strongly that it should be right for the deceased, right for the religion and right for the community and that this should be delivered consistently at the right time for all patients. Eventually, responsibility for handling deaths for faith communities was transferred to chaplains, drastically reducing the level of complaints.

In this role, Samuel was asked to spend the first few months building relationships with colleagues from senior to frontline positions to hear about people's experiences at the trust. From this, a values and behaviours programme was established, after which Samuel's focus became EDI. He wanted to set up a network but encountered resistance. Senior leaders were keen to hear staff views on the matter, and so a meeting was arranged and staff of ethnic minority background were invited.

The birth of the 'BAME' network

The network was to be a base from which staff could have a collective voice that could be used to share information and lived experiences and request changes to policies and behaviours that marginalized BAME staff or contradicted the trust's values. Colleagues felt that little had changed as a result of previous initiatives, such as the yearly focus group meetings where concerns about BAME experiences were raised but little was done to change these experiences. The resistance in the room was strong; however, an unexpected ally supported Samuel's call for a BAME network to be established and rallied attendees to agree to establishing a network. The CEO was informed, and the network was born.

Samuel and his co-chair worked together to get buy-in from allies and BAME colleagues and worked with the board to establish the network. The network provided a platform for people to come together for a common cause and was formalized with a Terms of Reference document that set out how the network would operate whilst being accountable to the trust board. For its launch, the network developed a trust board seminar that focused on lived experiences of BAME staff across the trust. There were emotional conversations and honest stories about people's experiences of working at the trust. One story moved board members to tears, as an individual narrated her experiences of not being provided with reasonable adjustments during her pregnancy, which led to a miscarriage. She was not given any support during her pregnancy and was informed that she would need to use annual leave to attend her maternity appointments, despite her manager being aware of her ill health related to her pregnancy and a white colleague who was also pregnant being given time to attend appointments. She raised this with senior management teams to little avail. After falling pregnant a second time, she decided it was not worth risking her own health or her child's and left the organization. Hearing such stories had a powerful impact on the directors, who shared their experiences of hearing stories from BAME staff and the improvements that needed to be made with senior leaders in the trust.

As a result of the first powerful listening event, the board held BAME network board seminars biannually to support the network and to ensure accountability for what it achieved. The network quickly grew and got a hundred members in the first few weeks. To build momentum amongst new members, monthly meetings were held to introduce the network, its purpose and how people could contribute. It provided a safe space to voice issues, seek advice or network with other members. It was a monumental year of progress, and the achievements within that first year included:

- establishing a BAME network with direct accountability to the board
- holding the trust's first ever WRES seminar: an event of storytelling, senior BAME leaders discussing race and a board action plan for the future
- holding a second WRES trust board seminar day
- agreeing to have trust board WRES seminar days every six months
- agreeing WRES training for heads of services and managers
- agreeing review of training on WRES to maximize impact
- developing relationships with the communications team, which released a detailed briefing in response to the Public Health England (PHE) review on the daily Covid-19 briefing; agreeing to have a WRES profile and section dedicated to race equality issues on future communications
- leading on risk assessments for BAME colleagues in response to the disproportionate impact of Covid-19 on BAME communities

- appointing a BAME lead to attend Covid-19 executive huddle meetings, a senior meeting where executives would discuss trust business; having a BAME representative who supported initiatives and ideas to be put in place to support staff
- appointing a BAME lead to attend the Covid-19 executive strategic group to support the direction of the trust and its response to the pandemic
- appointing another BAME lead to the Covid-19 workforce group meetings
- advising the board on how to address BAME concerns during the Covid-19 pandemic
- supporting BAME webinars held by the CEO and director of workforce to address concerns
- appointing a WRES lead expert, trained by NHS England, to be a race expert for the trust
- developing a risk assessment guidance workshop for managers to ensure confidence in completing BAME risk assessments
- appointing non-executive directors (NEDs) to champion EDI at board level; this evolved to board members becoming champions for each of the protected characteristics
- developing regional links with the Integrated Care System (ICS) network to provide advice, support and opportunities for leadership and development
- increasing the trust targets to increase BAME representation in leadership, which was formalized through the trust's workforce plan
- being involved in the planning and delivery of RCN BAME leadership training to deliver sessions along with the CEO, director of workforce and director of nursing
- supporting staff through career progression, discrimination and grievance cases

- having input in the regional executive agenda for race equality via the regional network
- being invited to attend the executive Task and Finish Group for Risk Assessment; this contributed to setting up webinars for BAME staff, designing risk assessments and supporting under-represented colleagues who otherwise felt they did not have a voice
- delivering WRES training for heads of services during a leadership forum with the CEO
- being involved in consultations at the request of trust and board leaders to discuss race equality
- being appointed to the executive social distancing strategic group and advising on matters like how social distancing could be maintained for prayer spaces for staff.

As the network continued to establish itself, the Covid-19 pandemic hit. The biggest challenge for Samuel during the pandemic was listening to stories of staff being treated differently during that time. Staff spoke about being left on the frontline and wearing masks for too long, which caused asthma exacerbations, because they were rotated last and white colleagues were given breaks first. He heard about staff reporting their co-morbidities to managers but nothing being done to help them manage their health needs, leading to ill health. Samuel recalls a doctor in tears who felt he needed adjustments but was not given them by his managers. The reason given for this was, 'If we make adjustments for him, then others might ask for them too.' The doctor was fearful and anxious, confiding that this was affecting his mental health and he was crying alone at night due to the stress this was causing him. The lack of basic compassion was tough to observe, and Samuel demanded that this staff member be given reasonable adjustments immediately. Occupational Health services had not been consulted for advice as per the protocol and the staff member had not been referred to them either for guidance. Unfortunately, no decision was made. The next day, the staff member called in sick, and all the stress he had held inside himself imploded, leading to a six-month absence from work. On his return, he still did not feel safe or secure and made the decision to leave altogether.

This colleague was a national authority in his field, a well-respected and capable doctor. The trust therefore lost a valuable colleague. Samuel had built strong relationships with colleagues across the trust and found this time difficult, as staff held him responsible for the outcome of risk assessments once they started to take place. Risk assessments were completed by the occupational health department, and when they concluded that no interventions were required after reviewing staff health, co-morbidities and risk of exposure against the protocols, staff would contact Samuel in frustration, blaming him for them feeling scared and unsafe at work. The lack of appropriate PPE at this time also caused fear and anxiety in people, who became increasingly frustrated at not feeling like sufficient measures were being provided to protect from the rapidly spreading disease. Whilst risk assessments took some time to introduce from when the pandemic first started, the trust had no guidance other than the already-distributed national guidance, which colleagues felt provided limited intervention from protecting against Covid-19 exposure. Samuel recalls sitting in a senior meeting to request that staff conduct risk assessments for BAME colleagues due to the disproportionate impact that Covid-19 was having on them. The questioning lasted for 45 minutes, during which Samuel was asked to explain why the risk assessments were important. Finally, the deputy director challenged everyone, 'Do you realize that we, who are all white, are asking the one black staff member why we as a trust need to find a solution for this issue?' This happened at a very early stage of the pandemic when the disproportionate impact of Covid-19 on BAME staff had not been fully acknowledged, but BAME staff knew that something was wrong and did not know who to voice their concerns to or what could be done. As BAME staff did not have a strong voice, the network hosted a meeting with the CEO to provide a safe space for staff to be able to raise their concerns. The meeting brought up a whole host of issues around the importance of BAME representation in senior leadership and the impact this had on staff. A nurse voiced his fear at seeing the number of BAME patients being admitted with Covid-19 and raised his concerns of not feeling like he was understood or heard by his senior management because they were not experiencing what he felt.

Despite the challenges he faced during the Covid-19 pandemic, Samuel is grateful that his CEO and director of workforce supported him in his approach to managing EDI issues during the pandemic. For example, he delivered a webinar to 120 senior management colleagues to educate them on the disproportionate impact of Covid-19 on BAME communities. Although Samuel and the co-chair of the network stepped up to deliver this, he felt there was little appreciation of what this work entailed at the time. Samuel worked in chaplaincy, and his co-chair worked in IT services. Neither had public health education, but they worked in the NHS fulfilling non-educational and clinical roles. What drove them to lead this webinar and the trust's response to BAME staff during the pandemic was hearing the fear and experiences of their colleagues and feeling moved to do something about it. The two spent hours of their time outside of work reading up on the topic, attending webinars and designing a webinar to discuss this issue. Whilst the commitment was commendable, it highlights the issue of departments such as HR and occupational health not understanding the diversity within their trust and acting on it. To resolve this, organizations should ensure that sufficient time and resources are allocated to addressing this important issue.

Challenges with leading a network

The above scenario highlights the vital role that staff networks can play in NHS trusts despite the stigma that can be associated with them. When Samuel set up his first BAME network, a colleague warned him, 'There goes your career.' There can be a stigma around leading networks due to the politicized nature of the role and the stress and burnout that come with it. Samuel continued anyway, remaining dedicated to a cause bigger than himself. Faith can be a driving factor for some, and Samuel describes it as being what anchors him to the core value of respecting others. Unless you strive for a cause for the betterment of everyone, you can end up producing divisions and inequality by only thinking about your own interests.

Leading the network has been tough at times. Samuel has been accused of being a 'coconut' (meaning black on the outside and white on the inside) by fellow black colleagues for 'covering up' what the organization is doing when they have raised a concern. As EDI lead, he is responsible for developing the action plan for colleagues to implement, but it can take time for change to be delivered. He describes his frustration at attending meetings where little action is taken to deliver on the agreed plans to improve race equality. At times, impostor syndrome kicks in, but Samuel takes a proactive approach in understanding the environment he operates in. He takes the time to understand his colleagues and their motivating factors and how he can align with these so that they can work together to support their ambitions as well as his own. It is important to him to treat everyone in the right way – with the utmost respect, culture and best of language. Fairness features heavily in Samuel's conduct, which he hopes will translate into the culture of the organization in which he wishes to see improvement.

As a chaplain, Samuel was questioned about why he was reviewing diversity issues. His response was that even within faith there is diversity. He strives to serve and represent all cultures, backgrounds and people. An example of this was sourcing a budget to support the Friday prayer space for Muslims. This space overflowed every week, so staff and patients were having to pray outside in the corridors, leading to space management issues and the lack of a respectable and dignified space for prayers. Samuel asked the CEO, 'If staff have to pray in the corridors, how does this demonstrate that you value them?' Samuel contacted the Muslim chaplain and asked what could be done to improve this. It was agreed that delivery of multiple Friday prayers by different imams would be supported, which led to a better staff and patient experience. For Samuel, it should be a key principle for any organization to support employees by understand and meeting their needs appropriately. In the NHS, it can be challenging to find widespread examples of this, despite the statement of the first constitution detailing 'a wider social duty to promote equality' (Department of Health and Social Care, 2023).

The NHS constitution can only work to the fullest when the communities that people come from are involved in the delivery of the NHS. The annual NHS Staff Survey analyses what percentage of staff have experienced discrimination from staff (8.3%) and patients

(9.0%), and there is little difference between the two percentages (Survey Coordination Centre, 2023). It seemed surprising that staff experienced a similar amount of discrimination from other staff members as they did from the general public; however, Samuel rightly points out that staff are products of the same community that patients come from. Community divisions can play out in organizations, especially if the organizational culture does not implement or demonstrate strong caring values and an open culture.

One of the challenges in organizations can be the close relationships maintained by certain people. Ethnic minority staff are often excluded from the 'shadow culture'. When jobs become available, they aren't informed or selected, and they are not given the opportunity to develop. This leads to disengagement from the system, low morale and little sense of belonging. Those who can will move on to the next workplace where they feel valued, but not everyone has this option, whether for personal or practical reasons, such as not having access to a car to travel further for work. They may continue working in their organization but are disengaged and don't particularly feel appreciated or respected, leading to lower participation in the workplace. A culture of nepotism can stop people from speaking up for fear of being labelled and future employment prospects being hindered. Whilst we can work on changing some of the metrics within organizations, the culture also needs to change to manage such behaviours.

Culture change and race equality

Culture change is one solution to the problem of race equality; however, there is not a one-size-fits-all solution. Racial inequalities are a 'wicked problem' in that one solution to resolve the issue may bring up other challenges. Even amongst allies and supporters, disagreements can arise. Whilst Samuel had a supportive CEO, there were times when they disagreed on approaches that the organization should take. For Samuel, it comes down to, 'Doing nothing is not an option.' In the space of race equality, if no one has a vested interest then the work is likely to be less effective. The downside of this is that whilst working in EDI can be rewarding, emotional taxation of the role is high, often leading to higher rates of burnout compared with other professionals (Pemberton and Kisamore, 2023).

Samuel describes sometimes needing to divorce yourself emotionally from the work. It can be frustrating when you are trying to maintain a reputation and role of improving culture, experience and metrics but are not getting anywhere due to being reliant on others to play their part. Samuel manages this by having various other interests, including being a trustee for a university. He enjoys this because he partakes in supporting other issues that the university is working through and not just race equality, providing some mental space from constantly dealing with the issues surrounding EDI. The challenge of getting trusts to recognize and willingly address race equality nationally can be tough. Whilst the work is necessary, Samuel says he is not intending to work in this area for too long due to the impact of the emotional taxation and burnout effect it can have. To maintain the succession pipeline of effective EDI leads, organizations should ensure that clear action plans and strategies are put in place, with individuals who are interested in and capable of supporting the agenda being supported to do this so that the work continues regardless of who takes the lead position.

The culture of the trust is not so dissimilar to the culture of the area in which an organization resides. This is where politics and national discourse around race and culture play a part. The narrative at the top filters down to communities and people and then plays out in a public setting, whether that is the workplace or the streets. Saying that, seeing brave leaders speak up where necessary provides some hope. For example, in response to Steve Barclay's letter to partnership leads saying that EDI teams should be disbanded (Taylor, Mortimer and Walter, 2023), partnership leads and the chair of the NHS Federation wrote open letters to Barclay describing his decision as inappropriate, divisive and not serving the interests of healthcare for employees or service users.

Samuel recalls discussing Barclay's letter with the Chair of NHS Federation. He reminded Samuel the first BAME network he set up several years ago was created in a more hostile climate than the one we face today. At that time, race equality was little spoken about, and things have changed since then. The topic is championed regionally, and some organizations have a relentless approach to adopting race equality, as outlined later in Chapter 11. Whilst there is global and national variance on this topic, and the rest of the world might not be where we are, his question was: Why can we not do what we have done before when we have the passion and belief to do so? There is a cost to health and wellbeing; this affects our impact, so it matters. The change for Samuel personally is also illustrated with his role as EDI lead. His predecessor had made little progress in addressing key EDI issues, which Samuel was able to significantly make key differences.

It is so important to acknowledge wins as you go along. Two years ago, when Samuel took over the EDI leadership, people with disabilities were half as likely to be appointed to roles as those without disabilities. Now it is equal parity of appointment to roles. The Investors in People award commented on how EDI work has influenced the way people feel in the organization, which was previously unheard of. A thriving network and a growing number of BAME people fulfilling senior roles means that the organization is slowly changing and making progress along its journey of race equality. However, there is still a way to go in terms of seeing national improvements. The questions below may help you to reflect on your journey and what can be done to support networks.

Reflective questions

* Do you have an interest in another area of the NHS? Write down your areas of interest. Arrange to meet someone from your area/s of interest or ask your manager for support to arrange shadowing in that area. See what the opportunity brings for you.

* Are you part of the race equality network? Could you offer your skills, experience or time to support the network?

* Can you develop a specific, achievable and realistic plan to achieve what you want in your career?

* If you are involved in running a network, write down what you have achieved so far and what changes you wish to see in the next year. Who could support you to achieve your goals, and how can they help?

— CHAPTER 6 —

Case Study 4: The Chief Executive Officer

This chapter will discuss:

- the role of the chief executive officer (CEO)
- BAME representation at CEO level in the NHS
- the impact of racism as it filters through organizations
- a sense of belonging and why this is important in the workplace.

While most people are aware that CEO is the top role in any NHS trust, they are not always aware of what CEOs do. This is a role that demands accountability, professionalism and leadership throughout the good and bad times that the NHS weathers. It is predominantly occupied by staff of white ethnic background, with 88.7 per cent of senior managers being of white background (NHS Workforce Statistics, 2022). In the last few years, we have seen a small increase in the number of CEOs who are black or Asian. Salma Yasmeen, who has recently been appointed as the CEO of Sheffield Health and Care NHS Foundation Trust, is the first known Asian and Muslim female CEO to lead an NHS trust. NHS CEOs can work in various capacities: managing ICBs, other service providers, mental health trusts, community providers and secondary care providers. Whilst there has been an increase in the number of BAME CEOs across the NHS, which is promising, there is still a way to go before this number is statistically representative of the BAME population in the UK and there is an equitable experience of the role.

Some CEOs I have worked with have described their role as being to serve staff and patients alike to ensure the best possible experience is provided for all. Officially, CEOs are financially and managerially responsible for the trusts that they oversee. It can therefore be a hugely challenging role that involves dealing with complex problems daily. The job is very stressful and is not as well paid as the private sector. It is described as being a hugely rewarding role, with most CEOs citing making a difference to patients as one of the top reasons why they do the role (Pitcher, 2015). The top three skills that CEOs demonstrate are strong resilience, an ability to inspire others and make decisions, and people skills that mean they can engage with others. The ability to lead large complex organizations through transformational change is required for the role, as are excellent skills in stakeholder management, developing people and delivering on targets and outcomes. One must be naturally collaborative and able to work with a variety of people, and being naturally inclusive is therefore essential (NHS England, 2021).

Research on the employment experiences of CEOs is limited; however, Timmins' interviews with CEOs provided insight into some of the challenges faced in the demanding role (Timmins, 2016). The main issues reported from CEOs were financial challenges that the NHS faces and the burden of over-regulation and inspection. The various and conflicting demands from different stakeholders were also challenging, and CEOs who were keen to improve patient services reported that this hampered their ability to lead change. Complaints about a bullying culture were prevalent, with some CEOs declining to be interviewed because their experiences of being bullied while working as CEOs still felt too raw to recount.

In 2018, around a third of CEOs were of a clinical, predominantly nursing, background (NHS Leadership Academy, 2018). The NHS Leadership Academy's case studies report identified the existence of barriers preventing progression into senior NHS leadership positions, with gender inequalities persisting, mainly impacting women. Despite this, a 2019 study evaluating the role of female CEOs in healthcare found that women CEOs have a clear inclination for developing patient-centred organizations, even in the most demanding circumstances (Silvera and Clark, 2021). The recommendation from this study was for hospital boards wishing to improve patient experience to consider promoting women to executive and CEO roles.

The average CEO tenure in 2018 was just three years. For such a complex and challenging role, which needs time to be able to deliver meaningful change, this is a rather short tenure. The future pipeline of successors for CEO positions was a concern following research identifying the short tenure of CEOs in the NHS, therefore various initiatives led by NHS England have focused on improving the talent pool and pipeline of CEOs. Diversity in ethnic representation remains low across NHS trust CEOs, with 8 out of 217 CEOs reportedly being of ethnic minority background (O'Dwyer-Cunliffe and Russell, 2020). There are regional differences in ethnic minority representation on NHS boards, with some regions demonstrating an increase and some a decrease (NHS England, 2023). Interestingly, in 2020 Birmingham still had no representation amongst executive directors in its five NHS trusts despite having a high BAME population of 40 per cent (Thomas, 2020).

The NHS Leadership Academy runs leadership programmes to support leaders looking to move into more senior roles. A specific programme for aspiring CEOs is available for senior colleagues. Other senior level programmes include the Nye Bevan programme, designed for senior leaders looking to move into their next board role (NHS Leadership Academy, 2023). Applications for all leadership programmes are encouraged from under-represented backgrounds, with specific programmes for BAME colleagues looking to progress into leadership or senior management roles.

At one point, Owen, the first black CEO of Calderdale NHS Trust, was one of only four black CEOs in the NHS. He is a keen advocate for tackling health and racial inequalities, having based his thesis on the challenges of increasing BAME representation amongst CEOs in the NHS.

An important point to note here is that whilst BAME representation is low in the NHS at executive and chief executive level, there is not much difference in other sectors of employment in the UK. Green Park's analysis of BAME representation in senior roles in the UK found that in the sectors of law, police, security, arts, culture and sport, there was only *one* BAME leader (Smith and Garcia, 2020). Just 4.5 per cent of the senior roles in the UK are held by BAME people (*ibid.*), despite being 18 per cent of the UK population. From 2017 to 2020, BAME representation in senior roles increased by just 1 per cent (*ibid.*). Only two of the FTSE 100 CEOs were from an ethnic minority background, and there were no BAME CEOs in the top UK financial institutions (*ibid.*). Although representation is slowly increasing, based on the current trajectory, the UK will not achieve a representative proportion of 18 per cent of senior roles being held by BAME people until at least 2044 – by which time, a fifth of the UK population is expected to be of ethnic minority background.

A second point to note about BAME representation is its need to reflect the lived experiences of the various communities that make up the UK. Having lived experience amongst senior roles and board-level positions provides insight into the nuances of different communities (Subramaniam, 2021). Empathy cannot always replace lived experience, which supports with building trust, representing those who are under-represented and building relationships. The expectation is that having lived experience amongst senior roles means that services are better suited to communities, thereby bringing better engagement, as people can relate to the services.

Growing up, Owen's family was one of the very few black families on a majority-white council estate. After leaving school, he secured a job as a deeds filer at a building society. Owen valued education and continued to study part-time alongside his full-time work. His passion for education was such that even as a CEO, he was still studying towards his thesis. He felt that it was important to progress in academia and was keen to develop by furthering his education independently. It wasn't enough to be good at the job; he felt that he needed to do something extra to stand out.

Being a strong believer in working out of one's comfort zone, Owen encourages people to think about working in the 'stretch' zone. This is where you apply yourself to doing something different, perhaps not knowing what the outcome will be but trying it to see what happens and what you learn from it. It is easy to get stuck in one's comfort zone, but it does not help you to grow or apply yourself if you remain comfortable. If you stay in your comfort zone, it means that when change occurs you are less able to adapt because you did not challenge yourself in the first place. When it comes to BAME experiences, it can sometimes feel as though career ambitions and progression are being restricted or blocked, as shown in some of the experiences narrated in this book. A common theme is individuals feeling held back from their ambition; Owen's advice on this is to think outside the box. There is always a way to change something, whether it is changing roles, arranging training or networking with others who may be able to help you to grow or find opportunities.

Sometimes, as BAME colleagues, we can get caught up in thinking our value is tied to the roles we have, especially when we work in a tough environment. It can become all-encompassing to think constantly about how to improve. However, the best thing to do is to take a step back and evaluate. Reflect. Staying in the one-dimensional mindset of viewing yourself from the perspective of your job role can lead you to undersell who you are as a person. As an individual, you have interests, skills and talents, some of which you may be aware of and some of which you are yet to discover. It is therefore important to think about yourself as a whole person and not just the person you are in the workplace. Taking on other roles outside of work can help with building experience, skills and networking. Going that extra mile to do something different may feel challenging at first, but it generally opens doors and brings skills and experiences. It is the people who go the extra mile to develop and enhance themselves who fare better. And in doing so, you'll often find that you meet other people who bring other opportunities.

Networking

One of the benefits of expanding one's circle through taking on other opportunities (whether that is volunteering, shadowing or learning a new skill or hobby) is networking. Through networking, you meet other people and enhance your circle. Networking can seem daunting to begin with, and in some cultures, it isn't something we think we know how to do. Networking can be as simple as having a meaningful conversation with someone. It could be reaching out to someone you haven't met before to ask for shadowing or a volunteering opportunity. It could be asking whether anyone has any roles that would be suitable for your skillset or development. You can also enhance your network and discover new opportunities by using social media platforms, such as LinkedIn, which is a useful tool for professional networking and development.

There is an assumption that extroverts find it easier to network, engage with new people and have conversations. For introverts, it might be a little more challenging. However, we are often a blend of the two, and it is important to learn how to flex between both whilst recognizing what your natural preference is, i.e., whether you prefer to be an introvert or extrovert. You may well find that you have different preferences in different circumstances and situations. The people who develop well are the ones who can recognize both skillsets (being introverted and extroverted) but use both as and when the situation dictates.

Equality or equity?

For leaders, recognizing individual preferences amongst colleagues is important, as is ensuring that different preferences are accommodated. This supports getting the best out of individuals by including them and understanding their preferences. We often hear the term 'equality, diversity and inclusion' (EDI) in relation to race equality. Owen's preferred word out of the three is 'inclusion' or 'inclusivity', because equality is not the same as achieving equity. Equality can be defined as a situation in which everyone receives the same treatment, and this does not always work for everyone (Cambridge Dictionary, 2023).

Equity better serves people of different backgrounds and needs. Equity differs from equality in that it recognizes that everyone does not start from the same place and acknowledges that where there are imbalances, these should be adjusted for (National Association of Colleges and Employers, 2023). By recognizing the different characteristics of people who make up British society, the Equality Act 2010 suggests that equity should be considered for different populations, even though it does not explicitly state this. An image that is often used to demonstrate this has three people of different heights watching a football game over a wall. One person is tall enough to see over the wall and does not require adjustments. The second person is standing on a wooden block (an adjustment to support 'equity') so they can see over the wall. The third person has been given two wooden blocks to stand on so that they can see too. These adjustments mean that everyone can see the football game without any barriers. Whilst this is a simple image, its sentiment is powerful. In another version of that image that demonstrates equality, each person is given one block to stand on, meaning that the first two people can see, but the third person cannot. One may well say that the complexities and nuances of society and healthcare are not quite as simple as the barriers in this image. However, we must start somewhere, and this image's depiction of equity is a start. (Readers can google 'equality vs equity image' to see this for themselves.)

As leaders, we are responsible for how inequalities are managed, because we are responsible for ensuring that everyone under our leadership has the means to achieve their full potential whilst being supported to thrive. Reflecting on one's leadership style is essential, and ensuring it remains inclusive must be a key theme in our conduct. Whilst equality and diversity are often mentioned along with inclusion, diversity may not always be representative of the people within a service or team. There could well be a BAME person in a role, but if lived experience of those who are unrepresented is not considered in decision-making and service delivery, the impact is limited. Statistically, ethnic minority populations are more prevalent in poorer parts of the UK. Populations from more deprived areas of the UK tend to be significantly higher users of the NHS, particularly emergency care (Mallorie, 2024). An interesting question for many who perhaps don't know what the lived experience of individuals from deprived backgrounds is like is: how well placed are you (or have you been) to understand the challenges impacting their health? Evidence-based research is important, but without the understanding of people's context through understanding their lived experiences, it has a limited impact.

To achieve inclusion, people need to feel that they are part of the bigger picture, whether that is in a team or a service. Their individual needs and background must be accommodated and respected to ensure the best possible potential is supported in that individual. Sometimes the focus can be on our differences and how these are accommodated instead of on what we need or want and how to provide it. Owen emphasizes the importance of modelling servant leadership, with a common question he asks being, 'How can I best serve you?' It is a question that sparks contemplation in individuals as they ponder what is required. Modelling servant leadership empowers individuals to define what they want and need, ensuring that they feel confident that they are being included. Sometimes there is a significant focus on who someone is; this may well be a question that some people are still exploring, so they can feel unsure about how to respond. Leaders would benefit from ensuring that we provide equity in the conditions that support a person to thrive instead of focusing on the differences between people. A simple way of doing that is asking, 'How can I best serve you?' or, 'What do you need in order to help you succeed?'

Some leaders may find it difficult to let go of the control they have over others. A tendency to lead from the front can develop. At times this is required in the form of directive leadership, but most literature on leadership establishes that providing others with the tools for success and allowing them to own that is better than leading from the front. A common interview question for senior leadership roles is: how have you achieved a major service user or patient outcome by leading from the back? This is a question Owen asks too, because it is important that leaders allow others to lead forward to effect positive change. When leading others, one must ensure they are getting the best out of people by providing the conditions that mean they can thrive.

Leadership can be tough, as it comes with responsibility: the leader is the main face of an organization and therefore holds the power to effect change. How does one individual who is responsible for all the employees take on the task of instilling change in others? Achieving this when leading large organizations is no doubt a large feat, and it can be challenging at times. Owen describes how, even as CEO, his role is limited due to his capacity as a single individual. One individual can only attain so much physically; therefore, it is important to build up those around you so they have the correct skillset to effect change. Sometimes there is an assumption that if someone takes on a management role, they know how to manage people. We promote clinicians into managerial roles, and their experience can no doubt provide a benefit, as they understand what service delivery in healthcare looks like. But not all clinicians have the skills to manage people well. The skillsets of clinicians and managers are different.

The skills required to manage people must be learned, understood and applied, and they constantly evolve as the world advances. Thirty years ago, how people were managed was very different, as was the working environment. Today, there is a strong focus on digital skills – skills that the workforce did not require in the past. In the future, we will see the rise of artificial intelligence (AI), and we do not know what this will look like when it comes to managing staff and healthcare systems.

Ensuring that managers are supported to deliver the best work that they can is important, as is ensuring that they have access to the tools and resources required for this. To resolve the challenge of one person only being able to bring about so much significant change in others, Owen's organization has an internal leadership programme. This programme encourages leaders to consider their values and behaviours, and how they action these. The programme contains dedicated focus groups and face-to-face training. Enabling face-to-face delivery supports better interaction and engagement from individuals, after which follow-up sessions are arranged to encourage accountability. This is a step towards embedding a culture and behaviour amongst leaders and colleagues that supports them to support others to achieve the organizational objectives. Owen highlights the need to be consistent over a period and be almost obsessive about ensuring its continuation, as change does not occur overnight. This can sometimes be a challenge if people want to change something too quickly or develop 'shiny object' syndrome (when someone wants to change something new as part of their role). It takes time and repetition to make changes, and culture change takes time too.

What progress has been made?

Owen and I reflected on whether meaningful change has occurred in race equality in both the healthcare system and the UK. At times it seems like little progress has been made. It takes time and repetition to change something of this scale, particularly when it is systematically present and embedded in daily practices, behaviour and organizations. There can be a reluctance to change the status quo, particularly when some people benefit from it more than others. This has a draining impact on emotional and mental health, particularly for those working in the inclusion space. It is emotionally and mentally taxing and sometimes begs the question of whether anything has changed over the years.

It is helpful to compare how things were 40–50 years ago with where we are now, in 2024. My mother was born in the UK and went to school here. She lived through the 1970s when racism was overt and the norm. The moment that school finished, BAME children would run for the school bus to ensure they caught the first bus available. If they missed the bus and had to wait for the next one, they would be targeted and physically assaulted by white kids. As my mother shared these events from her childhood, she told me of one young boy who was Bangladeshi. This boy was beaten so badly one day that he ended up in intensive care. There were certain no-go areas for BAME children because of the danger of being targeted and beaten. It was not unusual to see signs outside pubs and houses saying, 'No blacks, no Irish, no dogs.' Politicians peddled racist narratives, such as Enoch Powell's 'Rivers of Blood' speech and the slogan that Conservative MP Peter Griffiths used to win the Smethwick seat in the West Midlands: 'If you want a [N-word] for a neighbour, vote Liberal or Labour' (Wilson, 2020). BAME people would be discouraged from applying for promotions and in some cases struggled to gain employment. Today this is less prevalent. However, we are seeing a rise in this behaviour becoming normalized whilst still dealing with the impact and effects of systemic racism.

So have we progressed or not? The situation has certainly evolved. And despite the challenges around representation, lived experience and overt racism, we have seen some improvement. A crude way of reviewing it is to say that being physically attacked because of your race is less common than it used to be. But it does still happen. And by no means should this be the only yardstick of progress. In healthcare, there was a time when BAME people were simply not present in any leadership spaces. A promotion to the next level was unheard of. However, this is slowly changing, and it is a marathon not a sprint. But when we reflect on subtle changes, for example, like seeing a black CEO who has been leading large NHS organizations for several years, we can see that societally things are changing even if this is happening slowly. Yes, the representation of BAME CEOs across the NHS is still significantly lower than it should be, but it is better than it was 20 years ago and so the journey continues.

Sometimes it does feel like an uphill battle, particularly when parts of the media favour a right-wing narrative and paint the addressing of race equality as a negative issue. The term 'woke' is seen a lot and is sometimes used as an insult to describe someone striving for social equity, inclusion and racial justice (Fenwick, 2021). The word 'woke' has received significant attention in the media, as the Conservative ex-home secretary Suella Braverman described efforts to tackle racism and increase diversity as 'wokeness' (Syal, 2023). She further criticized efforts to tackle racism in policing and healthcare, two areas where institutional racism is prevalent (*ibid.*). This is despite evidence that inclusion benefits people and societies that make up the UK and that it is particularly important after the Windrush scandal, which the UK Government was responsible for. Unfortunately, 'woke' is commonly used by certain politicians who say that standing up for race equality is 'wokeness' and should be stamped out. However, to ignore inclusivity or labelling it 'wokeness' is a failure of people who claim to represent others. Improving this is the responsibility of those, particularly those in positions of power, who see inequalities impacting people who make up the UK. What benefit does maintaining inequalities provide in accessing health and social systems? Maintaining inequalities in health and social care is one of the reasons why it can feel sometimes like we are going backwards in this journey; however, a different perspective is that it shows the desperation of those who wish to exclude the different communities that make up the UK and are clinging on to the status quo despite the changes being powerful and adoptable.

'Chilling' behaviour

Owen has been in senior roles for a long time. When he was growing up in the UK, racism was overt. As he progressed in his career, he noticed that it was more covert, more subtle. Sometimes it was so subtle that it could lead to an individual asking themselves if they had understood something correctly. In a recent example, a group of BAME colleagues asked senior leaders to make a commitment on racism. Only a few senior leaders had done this, and so in a meeting there was a conversation about whether it was possible. After the meeting, a colleague approached Owen to ask him to consider what it had felt like to be on the receiving end of his comments in the meeting. Now, one cannot make assumptions about the colleague's intentions. Owen says that the discussion left a 'chilling' feeling; in this context, 'chilling' is defined as 'the concept of deterring free speech and association rights...that appear to target expression' (Askin, 2009).

Chilling behaviour can have consequences. It targets expression, meaning that it may well make someone think twice before they speak up next time. It can impact one's confidence in speaking up about difficult issues or challenges. It can lead to self-doubt, impacting self-confidence and self-esteem. It can be seen as a subtle and nuanced form of covert racism, leading to the feeling of being gaslighted. And sometimes when it occurs, you question yourself. If you respond overtly, your experience may be denied by others, leaving you to ask yourself: was it me or did that happen? It can feel like you're fighting a losing battle, whether you respond or not. It may make someone who is early in their career question whether they should speak up and how to respond to such behaviour. As someone who is more experienced, Owen has a strong sense of values and commitment to his objectives and continues with his work. Challenging such behaviour becomes easier when one is more experienced in dealing with such behaviours and has achieved the power and influence within the workplace that often comes with senior roles.

It can be a struggle for student or junior health professionals to have the confidence to challenge such behaviour. Students' fears of being marked down by clinical educators and juniors' fears of their managers hindering their career aspirations are real, and this becomes an unfortunate reality for some. It can have devastating consequences for career aspirations, mental health and overall well-being. Leaders and healthcare providers should therefore reflect on how we deal with such behaviour that led to the 'chilling' effect. More so, we should be striving to develop organizational cultures that do not enable such behaviour to prevail in the first place. You might be asking which organizations would allow this behaviour, but we have seen an increase in staff feeling unable to speak up about behaviour that compromises patient and staff safety (Baines, 2022). Not feeling able to speak up can lead to declining staff morale, staff feeling unsafe, poorer patient experiences and reduced patient safety – all of which have serious consequences (Patient Safety Learning Hub, 2020). This environment fails to provide a psychologically safe space for someone to express their opinions or concerns confidently, which can lead to problems for patients and services. Ten years ago, the Francis report highlighted the fact that ethnic minority staff have a fear of speaking up for fear of being blamed (Francis, 2013). This is linked to patient safety and is something I touched on earlier in this book.

The physical and emotional impact of racism and discrimination

Sometimes, as BAME individuals, we develop a stoic response to negative behaviour. In some cultures, it is common to not show emotion or express our thoughts if we disagree with something. Rather than say something, we 'save face'. We stay quiet even when something occurs that we do not agree with. We may be angry or upset inside, but we don't show it. This can lead to us feeling like a sponge that absorbs such behaviour but doesn't let anything out. It can influence self-confidence, self-esteem and one's own mental health if we internalize such experiences. It can lead to people becoming increasingly frustrated but not challenging such sentiments or voicing their feelings. As such feelings build up internally, it can lead to outbursts and feeling burnt out. We may not feel confident to share our thoughts as openly as we wish to for fear of being judged. As I reflect on this, the term 'biological weathering' comes to mind.

Biological weathering is a geographic term originally used to describe the process that rocks undergo when exposed to the elements over a consistent period. External stresses, i.e., water, natural gases and organisms, have an effect on the rock over time, leading to it weakening and collapsing in response to the stressors imposed upon it. Over 30 years ago, Geronimus first coined the term 'weathering' to describe the effects of racism and discrimination in marginalized groups (Gupta, 2023). The stresses include racism, discrimination and microaggressions, which over time have an impact on the physiological makeup of an individual. This can take the form of increased blood pressure, lower immunity, poorer cardiovascular function and increased cortisol levels (stress hormones). It can impact maternal mothers, negatively affecting babies' birth weights and overall health.

It impacts core bodily systems including cardiovascular health, metabolic system and immune responses. The cardiovascular impact includes increased heart rate, higher blood pressure even when sleeping and greater fatty deposit in arteries associated with the stress response, which have been demonstrated to be higher in individuals experiencing racism and discrimination (Geronimus *et al.*, 2006). Metabolically, it can lead to changes associated with insulin resistance, thereby increasing the risk of diabetes (Wagner *et al.*, 2013). In terms of gut health and immunity, it leads to increased levels of inflammation and activation of the cortisol hormone – a stress hormone – resulting in altered immune function. This contributes to an increased risk of developing co-morbidities and being less physiologically able in fighting illness (Ajilore and Thames, 2020).

Geronimus's research demonstrated that in the US, black mothers were far more consistently exposed to racism and discrimination, leading to an increase in physiological responses internally associated with stress, increasing health problems (Geronimus *et al.*, 2006). In short, racism is making those who experience it sick. Her research was vehemently rejected when it was first published 30 years ago, causing her to retreat from speaking about this topic publicly. Public discourse has since evolved, and today her research is widely accepted. It paved the way for an honest conversation on the impact of racism and discrimination on those who experience it. Further research has since been conducted to review the effects of racism and discrimination in society. Although Geronimus's research initially focused on black and white Americans, further research has since reviewed the impact on other minority communities like Latino Americans and lesbian, gay, bisexual and transgender (LGBT) groups (Jarral, 2023). The findings are likely transferable to other countries that experience similar issues with racism and discrimination of marginalized groups, such as the UK. In the UK itself, a report published during the first year of the Covid-19 pandemic by Public Health England explicitly stated that systemic racism and discrimination played a part in the disproportionate impact of Covid-19 experienced by BAME communities during the pandemic (Public Health England, 2020).

Recent research conducted by the University of California Health explored the ways in which racism and everyday discrimination affect the body, reviewing its impact on the brain, stomach health and the immune system. Researchers describe how structural racism and everyday discrimination impact health negatively, including issues like obesity, diabetes, cardiovascular function, early birth, anxiety, depression and even suicidal thoughts (Schlossberg, 2022). Emotionally, it can lead to increased feelings of overwhelm, isolation and feeling withdrawn (Mind, 2021), which in turn can impact a person's overall state of health and wellbeing. In summary, racism can make you sick.

Articulating lived experiences is tough. And hearing lived experiences of racism and discrimination throughout the compilation of this book has been tough too. Owen spoke about how we sometimes come across white people who appear genuinely horrified at the experiences of BAME people in the UK. And there may well be some sympathy or empathy with the lived experiences that they hear. The true test of allyship is what that person does after they have heard such stories. Do they change their behaviour, or do they maintain the status quo?

I ended the conversation with Owen by asking what the toughest moments in his career have been. Owen has had lived experience of things not going the way that he had intended or making decisions that did not lead to a fair outcome. These situations make you stronger, more alert and more naturally curious. Owen recalled a time when one of the services in his trust was rated inadequate. This was a serious situation, and as he travelled to see the minister for health to discuss the issue, he was aware that the conversation would determine whether or not he would still have a career. Owen described what this situation meant for him: first, an ability to recognize that he was part of the problem – he was the CEO and therefore the accountable officer; second, taking ownership of the problem; third, the determination to put it right. He remembered a colleague's partner commenting that Owen was held to far higher standards than other individuals in the same league. This comes back to what you are grounded in – your values and your continuous development. Despite being 55 years old, Owen still undertakes mentoring and coaching for self-development. Owen recommended a book called *Why Should Anyone Be Led by You?*; for him, the key words from the book are, 'Be yourself – more – with skill' (Goffee and Jones, 2006, p.1).

We spoke about having a true sense of belonging in the workplace. I asked Owen, as a CEO, whether he feels a true sense of belonging and how he deals with it. Owen is of Jamaican background, and he reports that people can often be loud in Jamaican culture. He likes to listen to R&B music, but conversations about this will very rarely occur in leadership spaces. You become accustomed to responding to different environments and managing behaviours differently where our culture perhaps is not the mainstream culture. Owen sees this as a strength. But should this be the case? Should we, as ethnic minority individuals who make up the fabric of UK society, feel that we must 'hide' our identities in certain spaces? We agreed that this should not be the case, coming back to the word 'inclusivity' and how inclusive we are in our environments. Whatever job you are in, try to be brilliant at it; try to be fantastic at it. Not just good but brilliant. Aligning with one's own values supports this. Owen is driven by the impact he has on others. This needs to be balanced with ensuring that you look after yourself.

We spoke about the poorer experiences of colleagues in frontline roles. The change is not a linear process. It will be messy, and at times, steps forward will be made only for steps backward to be taken. Consistency is key. Whilst we are perhaps making some progress in terms of representation, providing support and psychologically safe spaces to support people through racism and discrimination is also necessary.

If we are not a part of the system, then how will we influence the change we wish to see? An old football commentator used to say that if you don't buy a ticket, how will you win the raffle? It is easy to walk away from it and surround myself with people who are just like me. But doing this plays into continuing systemic racism. I'm reminded of the idea that anything worth having is worth fighting for. The road to improving racial inequalities can seem tough and like a battle at times. But viewing it as a journey to attainment instead of a battle helps to shift the perspective.

Reflective questions

* What are your values? Have you considered these and how they may impact your professional life before?

* Are you where you want to be in your career? If not, what steps can you take to get there?

* Sit with a notepad and pen. Evaluate yourself as a person, i.e., your likes, hobbies, interests, career. See yourself as a whole person. Next, review the skills you demonstrate in your various roles. How can you use these to support your professional development?

* What do you currently do in terms of professional development? Can you identify any opportunities for shadowing or secondment to support your progression? If so, what steps will you take to achieve these opportunities?

— CHAPTER 7 —

Case Study 5: Clinical Support Worker (Band 3)

Clinical support workers support the NHS in the delivery of services, predominantly by looking after patients. They work at a band 3 level, with starting salaries of £22,816 (NHS Employers, 2023). Across the various NHS settings (i.e., hospital services, mental health, community services), there are almost 340,000 full-time clinical support staff. This means that the clinical support staff workforce is larger than the nursing and midwifery workforce combined (Palmer *et al.*, 2021). Higher level qualifications such as a university degree are not required but skills and training are expected, mainly in the form of care certificates. This is one of the bands where we see a higher representation of ethnic minorities.

This case study is of a band 3 clinical support worker. It is important to understand that the range of band 3 roles is vast. Band 3 roles exist across all areas of the NHS, including healthcare assistants on wards who support patient care. As technical instructors, band 3 staff work with AHPs to support patients in completing rehabilitation programmes. In pathology, band 3 staff support doctors and nurses with taking bloods and completing procedures for patients. There is a remarkable range of job titles, roles and duties that fall under band 3 roles, and this can sometimes contribute to role ambiguity (Jasper *et al.*, 2019).

In the corporate side of the NHS, band 3 roles provide the invaluable function of administration as secretaries, administrators, assistants or system support. The healthcare system would collapse without the band 3 staff. Whilst there is a requirement and necessity for highly trained healthcare professionals in the NHS, there is also a demand for our support colleagues, who are often undervalued. Band 3 colleagues may not be regarded as highly 'qualified', but they are still highly skilled in terms of the experience that they bring. Band 3s can train up into other roles and progress to leadership roles. I recall from my experience of working in the NHS a senior management colleague who first worked in the NHS as a therapy assistant, worked hard to become an AHP and then worked her way up to a senior management role. She had the experience and background of having worked in patient-facing roles throughout her career journey, which gave her an understanding of the issues related to the core business.

Clinical support workers work closely with nursing staff, who often provide supervision. A debate exists about the upskilling of band 3 staff and how this potentially impacts the role of nurses in managing patients. Historically, clinical band 3 staff have always worked under the supervision of a qualified healthcare professional. As demand of healthcare continues to outstrip capacity, band 3s find increasing opportunities to upskill and progress. For some nurses, this can be disgruntling. Qualified health professionals spend a lot of time, money and effort on obtaining a degree and then find that they do not experience the hands-on element of care, as this is seen as the role of clinical support workers. Sometimes there is a lack of clarity on what nurses and healthcare assistants should be doing and whether one is complementing or substituting the other (Wilberforce *et al.*, 2017).

The significance of band 3s was cited in a 2020 review led by Professor Sir Mike Richards, which recommended an increase of 2670 administration and band 2/3 support roles in imaging services alone (Richards, 2020). The report also acknowledged that other ways of growing the workforce include developing new roles, flexible and innovative working, and reviewing changes to education and training (Richards, 2020). As patient demand continues to outstrip workforce capacity in the NHS, encouraging employment retention in the healthcare system through the 'grow your own' workforce model, in which band 3s play a significant role, is seen as a workable solution (Health Education England, n.d.). Health Education England's workforce planning model is a well-thought-out guide for service leads that considers how to 'grow' the workforce. It provides advice on where to recruit employees externally so they are reflective of the communities served in the NHS. The model is dependent on providing apprenticeships and entry routes into the NHS so that staff can work their way up through the organization.

The ethnic makeup of band 3s nationally demonstrates an over-representation of black British people in mental health settings but this is not as significant in other areas i.e., hospital and community services. There is little research that reviews the experience of clinical support workers; most of the research focusing on lived experience of healthcare professionals is with qualified healthcare professionals. It amazes me that despite clinical support workers being the largest NHS workforce, there had not been more research to understand their experiences. As part of this book, I interviewed Rehana*. Rehana is a band 3 clinical support worker who has worked in the NHS for many years. She shared her journey with me, including what she has lived through and continues to endure.

Rehana describes herself as outspoken but down to earth and proud of her humble beginnings from a working-class town. Her father always told her to speak up for what is right, so she doesn't shy away from doing this. Throughout her working life, she has worked in various care roles and organizations, supporting the elderly, young people and disabled people. She describes herself as a 'people person' and likes working in care because she enjoys the interaction she has with others. Before joining the NHS, she changed jobs quite regularly, finding that she would get bored quickly in her roles. One of the factors that encouraged her to apply to work in the NHS was that the local hospital was convenient and easy to get to. As a single mother, working closer to home helped Rehana with the juggling required to raise a child and maintain a household while being employed.

She applied for a support worker role and was successful. She was relieved to be working closer to home and eager to settle into her new role. She enjoyed the patient contact and busy nature of working on the ward but felt she was treated differently by some of her colleagues. One colleague was a domestic worker, whose role was to provide food and drinks to patients and keep the wards clean. The domestic worker did not like Rehana offering drinks to patients and repeatedly told her that it was not her job to do this. Rehana noticed that this colleague had no objections to Rehana's peer colleagues – who were white – providing patients with drinks when they requested them. Rehana noticed that when ethnic minority patients asked for a drink, the domestic worker would say that they had to wait until teatime. However, if a white patient requested a drink, the domestic worker would give them the requested drink.

Other ethnic minority workers who experienced this behaviour did not feel confident in speaking up or addressing it because the domestic worker was friendly with the ward management team, so there was fear about what may happen to them if they spoke up. As the weeks continued, Rehana would raise this issue regularly with her supervisor, but little changed, and she felt ignored.

On one occasion, Rehana booked annual leave, which had been pre-authorized several weeks earlier. A few days before her leave was due, Rehana's colleague informed her that her leave had been cancelled, as another member of staff had requested annual leave for the same period. The member of staff who was being given leave was good friends with the supervisor, and the supervisor had cancelled Rehana's leave without informing her directly about it. Rehana found out when a colleague happened to mention it. Rehana told her supervisor that she was aware her leave had been cancelled but she had not been informed of this. She said that this was not appropriate, as she had not been consulted. Rehana was aware she could contact the union to resolve any issues and informed her supervisor that she would not hesitate to do this if the matter was not resolved. The supervisor agreed to resolve it by not cancelling her annual leave, and the matter was closed.

Rehana continued in her role, working enthusiastically to complete her care certificate to support her career development. She spent a lot of her own time furthering her learning to complete the certification, as well as using break times. At that time, care certification was new, and it took months to complete the certification. Rehana was proud of this, but she overheard some of her colleagues saying, 'She probably knows someone internal and that's why they have passed her.' Rehana told me that the colleagues making such statements would also ask her for her file so that they could use it to help with the completion of their care certificates.

The charge nurse was supportive of Rehana's career and commended her for being the only one on the ward to achieve 100 per cent compliance with her mandatory training. He offered to support her training and development to enhance her skills. As she reflects on this, she says that she believes she would not have progressed in her career without his intervention. In this role, the charge nurse was the only individual who took time to review her performance and training, and support her with further training to build her experience.

One day, while Rehana was working on the ward, an unwell patient required fluids. The patient needed a drink and Rehana made the patient a cup of tea to support their fluid intake. The domestic worker then came along and shouted at her in front of the team for making a drink. Rehana felt humiliated and left the ward in tears. She had wanted to help the patient by supporting their fluid intake, and the domestic worker had not allowed her to do this.

As she cried in the office, two of her managers came to see her. Rehana felt that if her earlier concerns about the domestic worker had been addressed, this situation need not have arisen. Her managers agreed she should go home, and the situation was swiftly resolved with the domestic worker apologizing and though she allowed Rehana to make drinks after that, she did not allow other ethnic minority staff to do so.

Rehana was keen to progress in her career and wondered whether working elsewhere might be more inclusive and friendly, so she applied for another role.

Rehana was successful in her application and looking forward to a better experience. However, she says that the grass isn't always greener on the other side, and her new role seemed even worse. The manager would hold team meetings for all staff but refuse to look at or acknowledge any ethnic minority staff in the team. BAME staff would sit on one side of the room and white staff on the other. Racial divisions within the team were evident. Any attempt by BAME staff to speak or provide an opinion on a matter being discussed would be refuted or ignored. Rehana describes how her white colleagues would constantly make racist comments to ethnic minority staff, including the following remarks:

- 'Your food stinks.'

- 'Why do they look like ninjas?' (Referring to women wearing headscarves.)

- 'I've just seen a patient and all I could see was her eyes.'
- 'I've just seen a patient who stinks of curry.'
- If black patients came to the ward, there were comments like, 'All I can see is their teeth and their eyes,' and, 'They smell.'

Staff made racist comments daily. Rehana would sometimes respond to this taunting by asking, 'Why don't you ask HR?' but little changed. There were a few other BAME staff members, and they did not respond to this behaviour. One of Rehana's colleagues informed her that an Asian colleague in the team resigned because she could not cope with the racist bullying any more.

One day, Rehana was called by her manager who told her that someone had claimed that a patient had complained about Rehana, stating that she had violated infection control policies for a procedure.

The manager asked for a response, and Rehana denied she'd acted as had been claimed. The manager explained that the complainant had made similar complaints in the past about other well-liked staff and they had then left. The taunting from colleagues continued, as did being ignored when it came to raising concerns and unfair shift allocation amongst the team.

Rehana also noticed that if her colleagues struggled with taking blood from a patient, they would not ask BAME colleagues to support them with the procedure. Instead, they would ask the patient to return. One day, she overheard a patient asking her colleague to ask for Rehana's help in locating a vein, but the colleague refused, instead asking the patient to return on another day. Not only is this a waste of resources and time for the patient, but it also begs the question of why they would not allow another colleague to attempt the procedure if they were skilled to do so.

Whilst working in this role, Rehana says she was never offered training, appraisal or supervision. After some time, she couldn't tolerate the situation any longer, so she applied for another role.

She was successful in her promotion. She joined a small team where she was the only staff member of ethnic minority background. Her shift pattern was agreed so it supported her childcare and financial commitments. But, a few weeks later, her shifts were changed.

Rehana noticed that one colleague was always abrupt with her and another did not like it when colleagues commented on Rehana's skills or helpful nature; for example, in supporting other teams in an emergency if they were short-staffed, she was accused of doing this just to, 'Get in the good books of the doctors.' Rehana denies this, explaining that she firmly believes she has a duty of care to support patients who require treatment and says that if she can offer support, then she will always help out.

One day, after one of her colleagues got angry and was unnecessarily rude and aggressive to Rehana in front of other people, Rehana and others present felt the colleague had also breached safety procedures and she later asked for an apology. When the colleague ignored this, Rehana reported the incident to her manager and to the matron on the Union's advice. The manager didn't formally respond, but when she bumped into Rehana one day simply told her that the incident didn't happen as Rehana claimed and tried to persuade her to drop the complaint, eventually pinning her against a wall and yelling in her face in a closed room. The situation ended in a mediation, where Rehana did receive an apology but the manager then asked Rehana why she had put her colleague through the stress of potentially being sacked. Rehana felt her humiliating experience continued to be underplayed, even after it had been admitted and apologized for.

After this, Rehana felt the manager showed the colleague favouritism, for example telling Rehana she couldn't go home early but had to take sick leave if she felt unwell, whereas the colleague was not required to do so and could leave early when unwell. When Covid-19 hit, Rehana was badly affected and was off work for several months. She felt unsupported on her return to work after this and another period of absence. For example, she was not trained on changes that had occurred in procedures, yet was publicly berated for not knowing about them.

She felt targeted by her colleagues. She decided that she was no longer going to contribute to the team by providing ideas and would focus on seeing patients instead.

The atmosphere at work was becoming increasingly hostile. Rehana could hear colleagues talking about her and saying, 'Don't speak to her or she will report you.' She was ignored in meetings and felt that the team was becoming increasingly unstructured. Being the only BAME staff member in her team and the only one subjected to such experiences meant that she felt that her race was a factor in how she was being treated.

She decided to go to the Freedom to Speak Up Guardian[1] but found that a difficult experience as when the guardian passed her concerns on, her matron told her that if she felt left out and ignored she should leave and she was dismayed to be asked to confirm she had mental health issues. Rehana informs me that whilst she does stand up for herself, this has an emotional impact. It creates fear and anxiety about going to work. She feels isolated due to the poor relationships with her colleagues and managers. A new line manager has refused to reply to her emails. She has now resigned herself to not putting her opinions forward about how things could improve for the service.

The worst experience Rehana describes, which she says still scares her even now, is when she was pinned against the wall. She wonders what would have happened if they had not been in an open space and whether others would have heard her if she'd screamed or what would have happened if there hadn't been another member of staff present. She wonders what would have happened if she had not had the courage to stand up for herself even in this frightening situation.

I ask her why she continues to work in a role that has brought her so many difficulties. She replies that whilst she has no trust left in her management or colleagues, as a single mother she has no one else to rely on to provide for her family. Despite the difficulties she experiences at work, she still says she loves her job and that the patients make her smile. Rehana is incredibly dedicated to her patients and to providing a good service. She loves the fact that no day is the same and that she meets new people every day. She speaks with pride about the challenges at work in terms of the patients she meets and procedures she completes daily. She says that 90 per cent

---

1 The Freedom to Speak Up Guardian roles were introduced to enable staff to raise concerns in a confidential manner at work. The guardians support staff members to address the issue. Staff members should be supported to raise concerns anonymously if they wish. The role was introduced following the Francis report in 2013, which highlighted that staff did not feel safe raising concerns for fear of being punished or criticized.

of her role has been horrible but 10 per cent is nice because of her patients, which makes it worth coming to work. As she prepares for her shift every morning, she worries about seeing her colleagues, which creates stress and anxiety. She does not have the energy to deal with her colleagues any more. She still cannot understand why her new manager will not speak to her or acknowledge her. She wonders where she has gone wrong. But she has resigned herself to the situation and says that it's not worth causing herself any extra stress and anxiety about what she faces with her colleagues, and she has decided to no longer speak up.

Rehana also works shifts on National Health Service Professionals (NHSP), another bank organization. It is common for healthcare professionals to work on the NHSP service, which serves as a 'bank' of staff who can work extra shifts when the service requires this. One day, she was working on a ward as a healthcare assistant, and ward staff kept making inappropriate comments. First, one of the healthcare assistants commented on her handbag and her clothes, saying that they were expensive and asking her how she could afford it. The same healthcare assistant then kept telling her what to do, even though they were all working on the same shift and there was no difference in clinical competency. Rehana became annoyed, telling the healthcare assistant to do some work instead of telling her what to do. As she exited the bay after finishing with a patient, the same healthcare assistant came up to her and shouted in her face. The tirade ended with the healthcare assistant walking away and shouting down the ward corridor to the nurse, 'If you don't get her off the f***ing ward, I'll f***ing kill her.' Rehana was concerned for her safety and voluntarily left the shift, no longer feeling safe at work. The nurse in charge did not resolve the issue, and Rehana emailed management to inform them of what had happened. Little came of this, and the issue was not resolved. Her faith and confidence that the system will support her career progression, her right to a safe working environment and her right to express opinions and ideas on what works best for the trust has been eroded.

Despite the poor relationships with her colleagues, Rehana is widely recognized across the theatres team and by surgeons in her trust, who know of her work and regularly send emails of praise to her line manager. She has good working relationships with wider colleagues. Rehana takes pride in supporting anyone in need, and she goes above and beyond to support colleagues when patients require urgent procedures that she can support. She proudly tells me that many doctors – from Foundation Year 1s (doctors who have newly qualified, also known as junior doctors) to registrars to consultants – comment on her speed, efficiency and clinical ability to complete procedures well. She is proud of her strong work ethic but feels that this is criticized by her team colleagues and wonders why.

Her commitment to her role despite her experiences is admirable, and hearing her experiences was emotional. Here is an individual who can offer so much more than she is enabled to in her workplace but feels defeated due to her experiences. Instead, she has resigned herself to coming in to do the job that she is paid for and then going home. She tells me that she is mentally and emotionally tired. Her final words were that as a person of an ethnic minority, you are not entitled to make changes or share ideas. Rehana's story provides a dark picture of what racism looks like in the NHS. Below are some reflective questions following this case study.

Reflective questions

* If you were in a similar situation, how would you speak up?
* How could Rehana look after her emotional and mental health in this situation?
* What would you do if you were in this situation?

Reflective questions for managers and leaders

* Consider the WRES indicators – which have been breached in the case study?
* How do you ensure that conflict is resolved appropriately in your team?

* If you are struggling to manage conflict between colleagues, from whom can you seek support to help resolve the issue?

* Is there favouritism amongst your colleagues? Do you feel confident in managing it?

* How do you ensure there is professional conduct amongst all members of your team?

* What is the culture of your team like? Is it in line with the values and behaviour of your organization? If not, how could you implement steps to change this?

CHAPTER 8

Allyship and Its Importance

The previous five case studies focused on the lived experiences of BAME individuals across the NHS in a variety of roles. Reviewing their experiences led me to consider what role the wider population plays in race equality. Striving for equity for all is not the responsibility of those affected by it but should be a collective responsibility. The fact that some people are treated differently because of their skin colour should concern us all. Whilst this book focuses on race equality in the NHS, this is a global issue that the global majority needs to work together to improve. It is not impossible for a small number of people to achieve change, and history teaches us that it can be achieved by a minority. But change becomes more influential and powerful when more people participate in it.

The earlier case studies discussed examples of initiatives that were implemented to support race equality. Initiatives like leadership programmes, race equality training and employing inclusion leads play an important part in raising awareness and breaking down barriers. However, true change comes from being open, curious and willing to have conversations with people within cultures that support being open, respectful and kind to others. The smaller daily interactions we partake in to discuss race equality and how we support people are what tend to make a bigger difference.

Mentoring is an enriching process. One of the reasons why I find mentoring powerful is because it is an opportunity to sit with someone and listen curiously to their experiences. When participating in mentoring, I actively listen and ensure that all other distractions are removed. I consider what my mentor is saying carefully and deeply, I reflect on how that makes me feel and what it means for them and I consider where my experience may have differed. It can be tough and uncomfortable at times, requiring a deep level of vulnerability, but having conversations like this has changed my career and personal growth. Ultimately, we are people before our roles. And when we break down the busy realms of professional life, underneath there is a human with emotions and feelings that we all experience, whether we are in touch with them or not.

In these confidential conversations, a psychologically safe space must be created to enable someone to be vulnerable and feel able to share experiences. This takes time, honesty and trust, as well as a leap of faith that while it may not be what you expect, it could provide you with so much more. Patience and reflective skills are helpful, as it takes time to build a relationship. You may find that you don't 'click' with a particular mentor. I would advise you to end the mentoring if you are not comfortable with someone, but make sure that you communicate this sensitively and respectfully.

Allyship and mentorship have some similarities: both involve having a level of vulnerability. I recall one of my earlier mentors sharing a difficult experience for the first time. I remember how uncomfortable it felt to hear about her experience and the range of emotions that came with it. But I learned from this experience, and it encouraged me to be kinder and more empathetic towards other people's experiences. In any organization, empathy towards people supports growth for everyone. After the conversation, I reflected on how our relationship had grown, because our first meeting was more of a formal discussion about my career aspirations than a conversation about challenging situations I had faced and the personal impact of these experiences.

Since race equality has been spoken about more over the last few years, many have claimed to be 'allies' and to champion equal rights for everyone. I have met with directors who label themselves allies and are striving for race equality, supporting public pledges to end racism in their organizations and signing up to reverse mentoring schemes. However, they do not respond when they are contacted after such pledges or they cancel their mentoring meetings without explanation, leaving their mentee confused. Such behaviour does not reflect a true commitment to allyship or race equality, and I am calling out this behaviour here because it is unacceptable. It does not provide consistency between what one says and what one does, and it is disappointing to experience and see. Allyship is not tested with words, it is tested with deeds and behaviours. It baffles me that people claim to be one thing publicly and behave differently in private. It is not reflective of the values we should be demonstrating in the NHS. Whilst there are different stages of allyship, as we will explore in this chapter, I don't think that poor responsiveness or doing little for the cause whilst publicly claiming to be an ally is reflective of a person who is striving for race equality with integrity.

The second part of this book will analyse allyship – why this is important and what it may mean for potential allies. Supportive ally relationships will be explored, allyship models will be reviewed and guidance on how one can become an ally will be provided. A variety of case studies from people at different stages of allyship will be detailed to show what allyship can look like.

What is allyship?

The concept of allyship has become popular in recent years, and in simple terms, it can be described as friendship. An ally is someone who is supportive of the cause but doesn't belong to a marginalized group. It is someone who is curious and willing to hear and understand people's experiences without judgement. It is a voice that supports others and champions the cause to raise awareness. It is someone who recognizes the privilege they have and helps to use that by supporting others who may not have that same level of privilege. It is developing relationships with people who don't look like you so that you can deepen your understanding of their perspectives and experiences, and using your newfound knowledge to do what you can to make the world (or the workplace) a better place.

Sometimes people ask what will happen to the mainstream opinion if we accommodate everyone's needs. The world is big enough for everyone's needs to be accommodated. It is selfish to suggest that your needs are not going to be met because an inclusive environment considers the needs of others who are less represented. Being inclusive doesn't take away your right, presence or ability to express how you feel or have an environment that recognizes your identity; rather, it extends that space for everyone instead of just serving the majority. It is a fragile mindset that thinks that, 'culture is being eroded,' because the needs of another group of people who look different to you are being accommodated. No one wishes to 'erode' culture; rather, various cultures can coexist and meet the needs of everyone. Differences should be met with curiosity, not with indifference. It is ironic that people feel this way, particularly when they fail to recognize that the UK went around the globe conquering other countries – at times being violent and leading to disastrous consequences – and don't seem to have an issue with the global repercussions of imperialism, such as the Great Famine of Ireland and the starvation of millions in India. This is one of the reasons why building relationships with allies helps us to understand perspectives that we may not have considered before.

The Cambridge Dictionary defines allyship as, 'The quality or practice of helping or supporting other people who are part of a group that is treated badly or unfairly, although you are not yourself a member of this group' (Cambridge Dictionary, 2023).

There are various definitions and meanings of allyship and what it involves. It will look different for every ally because allyship is an individual process that one goes through. In the next few case studies, each person has a different allyship journey. This is not a formal process, and one should not feel pressured to respond in a certain way to be considered an ally. There are some basic principles that define allyship, but one shouldn't necessarily feel that one has to identify as an ally to support race equality. I have met many people throughout my career who have supported race equality without publicly identifying as allies. Whilst social media plays a role in supporting movements publicly, not everyone is comfortable with expressing their views or actions on such platforms, but that doesn't mean that they do not support the cause. However, those who do support the cause publicly help to stimulate further conversations and influence others who may not be as interested in the matter or pay attention. And that is indeed powerful. We have seen through various movements, such as Black Lives Matter and #MeToo, that social media can play a key role in raising awareness, sharing information and influencing opinion, especially in comparison with the mainstream media.

Why is allyship important?

Allyship provides a helping hand for those who are marginalized or treated unfairly. In the NHS, racial inequalities have been prevalent for decades, and the earlier case studies demonstrate that whilst there has been some progress, there is still work to be done. There were examples of allyship in some of the case studies, such as Kiran's supervisor who supported her when her manager persisted in carrying out microaggressions. Allyship isn't always public gestures or statements; it can be quiet conversations to support co-workers in the workplace.

Allyship provides a voice to those who are otherwise unable to be heard and supports the empowerment of colleagues in the workplace (Shaikh, Lamar and Maguire, 2023). It can help others to rise through the leadership ranks and can support organizational outcomes. NHS trusts tend to set targets for increasing BAME recruitment at senior leadership levels, and allyship is one way of helping to achieve this target. This supports organizations to meet targets for organizational objectives. Supporting others who are struggling to progress can only mean improved efficiency and therefore productivity, which is a constant issue in the NHS that we are always working to improve. It can also positively impact staff retention and morale, and a happier workforce improves patient experiences, as discussed in Chapter 2.

Particularly when leading large organizations, it can be easy to think only from our own perspective as we deal with challenging problems that require urgent solutions. However, it is necessary to step back and review the bigger picture to see how our decisions will affect others, particularly those who may not have a voice. If we can't be open to hearing about others' experiences when we have failed them, either under our leadership or in our care, who are we claiming to serve? This is where allyship, self-reflection and emotional awareness are required.

Sometimes it can seem as though allyship is for a particular type of person. Social justice and race equality are applicable to everyone. They are not just problems for BAME individuals; they affect how we operate as a society. It is deeply prejudiced for a section of society to be denied the opportunity to progress because of supremacist thinking that they are perhaps 'lower' because of their colour. In the long term, this perpetuates unfair access to services and poorer experiences and is costly both financially and morally. Allyship therefore transcends all boundaries, people and levels of seniority. Each of us has a unique skillset, ability and talent, and there are people with whom we can work and whom we can inspire. Allyship begins with considering the basic principles outlined below.

What is the allyship model?

There are various models of allyship, and some active ways of practising allyship (Luthra, 2022) are listed below.

Deep curiosity: Curiosity is key to understanding experiences that are different from those you may already be aware of. Various factors influence the way we think, including our own experiences, historical knowledge, social contexts and biases we may have. When thinking of others who are different to you, make a conscious effort to understand their perspectives and experiences before thinking about how they relate to yours. Put yourself in their shoes as you wonder what it must feel like to live what they choose to narrate to you.

Self-reflection: Being able to understand ourselves is key to our own development. Reflect on yourself, your life and your achievements and consider how you make decisions. All of us have a level of bias, so explore what your biases could be and consider what this means for other people. This may well be an uncomfortable exercise, but this is how we grow and develop to overcome our biases and truly understand others.

Don't be afraid to say, 'I don't know': Being able to acknowledge that you don't know everything requires a level of vulnerability. And in the space of allyship, it is important to be able to listen to others without always seeking to provide a solution. You aren't expected to know everything, and when you listen to others, you can learn from their experiences. As you hear experiences that are different to yours, reflect on what that means instead of thinking, 'This doesn't apply to me.' And then consider what you could do to help someone through that, whether it is talking about their experience, signposting them to support or being able to change policy to support them and others who may be impacted.

Be empathetic in your approach: Sometimes, when we are listening to someone's story, we may place our own judgement on them without understanding what that experience means for an individual. Being empathetic with people to understand their narrative is likely to lead to people being less defensive or to the other person thinking about their biases without feeling judged. Sensitive questioning instead of blunt statements can help people to think about the impact of what is being said.

Listen actively when engaging with others: Being able to listen actively is a skill. We may think we are 'actively listening', but sometimes we are all guilty of planning an answer or a response to what someone has said before they've finished talking. This means we can end up switching off or not hearing the full story before we respond, which can lead to a breakdown in communication. Providing a psychologically safe space is important as an ally, as people may share difficult experiences. This can be done by listening actively to the person who is narrating their experience and not belittling them with comments like, 'Surely that didn't happen,' or denying their experience. Be careful not to dismiss what they are saying or be defensive; rather, listen openly and honestly, acknowledging that it may be difficult to hear but being empathetic to what the person is sharing with you.

Have a 'bias compass': Addressing one's own bias can be uncomfortable at times. It is important therefore to have a good network around you that can support you through understanding these biases, especially when they come to fruition in terms of decision-making or when engaging with others. Having a close, trusted circle that you can share ideas with before executing them is helpful and provides you with confidence to be more inclusive. Ensuring that the circle is diverse helps to support inclusivity. Having people who are already established allies or of under-represented backgrounds is helpful.

Be bold in taking ownership: Don't be afraid to start asking questions within your circle of influence. Observe who is and isn't represented within your circle. Asking yourself why your circle isn't representative is a good starting point. Seeking out people who are interested in helping to make changes could be a next step, including those whose viewpoint is missing. If you are aware of any colleagues who are under-represented and can help with a project, consider inviting them to meetings to support this. Not only will this provide a fresh perspective for the team, but it will also provide a learning opportunity for others. It could lead to opening a mentorship opportunity, which would be a great learning on the journey of allyship. Language is important, so consider what language is used across your team and how it could be adapted to be more inclusive.

What should potential allies do?

If you are considering becoming an ally but are not sure how to start, I would suggest starting with the points discussed above. Consider why allyship matters to you and the importance of tackling inequalities to ensure equity for everyone, particularly when it comes to healthcare. Be open and curious when engaging with others. Speak to allies that you know or reach out and have a conversation with a colleague who is an ally. You never know what you can learn from them, and you may find that they are more than happy to talk about their own experiences or point you in the direction of resources you can use. Speaking to people who are of BAME background in your organization can help too but be mindful that not everyone will want to share their experiences.

If you find a colleague who is happy to engage and talk about racial inequalities, listen without judgement to what they have to say. Ask questions and acknowledge their experience, validating it when you feel confident to do so. If you can and are able and confident to do so, amplify their voice if they are happy for you to do this. If they are not, ensure that you respect this, and explore whether you could support them in other ways. We may not always need to do something to 'fix' the situation, but providing a listening ear can help people feel like they are not alone. Contacting the REN for your organization can also support you in your journey, but bear in mind that networks may be at different stages of maturity. Some are well established, and some are starting out. Find out what stage yours is at and whether you can help. If the network has regular meetings, ask if you would be able to attend. Don't take it personally if you don't get the response you'd like, as it is about coming out of your comfort zone too.

The next three chapters contain case studies of allies who are at different stages of their journey. Understanding their different experiences reinforces the fact that no journey of allyship is the same. The reflective questions below can also help you think about allyship and where you may be on this journey.

> **Reflective questions**
>
> * How confident do you feel about being an ally?
> * Write down three actions you could take to commence your journey of allyship. Aim to achieve these within one month of writing them down.
> * If you are already an ally, reflect on what you have done so far. How could you continue to demonstrate your allyship or encourage others to do so?

— CHAPTER 9 —

Allyship Case Study 1: Being a Mentor

This chapter will discuss:

- what mentoring is
- the benefits of mentoring
- a mentor's journey in race equality
- how to improve race equality by supporting BAME staff.

We saw in the previous chapter that allyship consists of various activities that support race equality, with mentoring being one of the key activities. Mentoring is a process in which an experienced individual supports a less experienced person to help them with professional growth and development, although its personal benefits are also significant (Kline, 2009). It can be a spoken relationship or formally recognized, or you may find informal mentors in life who assist with any issues you may be experiencing. Mentoring schemes are quite common in the NHS; a dedicated hub is provided by the NHS Leadership Academy (NHS Leadership Academy, 2023) and several trusts run mentoring programmes. It is widely accepted, particularly in the corporate sector, that mentoring takes place to support learning and development.

There are various forms of mentoring, including one-to-one mentoring, group mentoring, peer mentoring and reciprocal mentoring (Sullivan, 2023). One-to-one mentoring is the most 'traditional' format and tends to take place over a period of perhaps 12–18 months, or even longer if both people wish to continue. Group mentoring has the benefit of being a setting that includes a variety of perspectives. Peer mentoring is like group mentoring, but it may not include a more experienced person to provide challenges or support with solving problems. It has the benefit of peer learning, which can lead to a more relaxed, open environment, as there may not be a hierarchical power dynamic present. Reciprocal mentoring is slightly different in that it is considered a two-way process of exchanging knowledge, skills and experience between two individuals, regardless of the seniority of the individuals in relation to each other (NHS England, 2014). There should not be a hierarchical relationship in reciprocal mentoring, although we may see executive directors or senior leaders taking part in reciprocal mentoring with junior colleagues to better understand their lived experiences, particularly those who are under-represented.

Mentoring provides many benefits for the mentor, mentee and organization. For the mentor, it provides an enhanced sense of job satisfaction, the opportunity to broaden their perspective and demonstrate their leadership skills, and the chance to use and enhance their existing skillset and abilities (Beheshti, 2019). It provides the chance to self-reflect and share experiences with the mentee, who benefits from learning from the mentor, and provides a sense of belonging through the commitment to someone in the organization. It helps the mentee to increase their network and self-confidence and to be open to new possibilities that they may not otherwise have been exposed to. Senior leaders reported that one of the top-three factors affecting their career growth was having a mentor (Abbajay, 2019). Benefits for the mentee include being able to support shadowing opportunities, identifying secondments for development or interest and getting the chance to be introduced to people who may help them in achieving their goals. For the organization, mentoring improves morale, job satisfaction and people feeling valued in the workplace by fostering closer relationships. It promotes positive role modelling of values and behaviours, and increases people's motivation to achieve their goals within the organization. In private companies, mentoring is commonly associated with better business performance, boosting productivity and attracting and developing talented individuals, with over 70 per cent of Fortune 500 companies running mentoring schemes for employees (*ibid.*).

Reciprocal mentoring schemes have been introduced across some trusts nationally (Health Education England, 2023). Benefits of these include better understanding of staff experiences, greater awareness of organizational context and developing relationships with under-represented colleagues (Raju et al., 2022). Whilst there is little research examining the role of reciprocal mentoring in the NHS, it is widely adopted, with anecdotal evidence suggesting that it is beneficial to those who partake in it.

Case study

This case study focuses on the story of Phillip, Executive Director for Workforce and Organizational Development at a large acute trust in Yorkshire. Phillip is a keen advocate for reciprocal mentoring, having taken part in the trust's reciprocal mentoring scheme on various occasions. Phillip is a proud Bradfordian, hailing from a diverse community with whom he shares his love for football as a Bradford City fan. Phillip regularly attended football games as a young boy, and in May 1995, he went to watch the Bradford City vs Lincoln City match. Phillip would ordinarily have sat in the main stand, but on this day he was late to the game. He usually sat with his father in F block, but it was full, so they had to walk around the ground to stand behind the goal instead. Little did Phillip know that this would be a blessing for him, as, tragically, a fire broke out in F block that day, claiming 56 lives. When Phillip left the ground, it was not known how many people had been affected or how badly.

A few years later, Bradford City football club was one of the first clubs that was about to be liquidated. Phillip felt strongly about the club, remembering those who had lost their lives in the fire, and wanted to ensure that the commitment of the club remained for the city. He enquired about whether there was a way of supporting the club to continue and was informed that a supporters' trust would need to be set up. He didn't know what a supporters' trust was at the time, but he volunteered to join the trust and became the vice chair. He was thrown into the spotlight, conducting live media interviews to explain what the trust was trying to achieve. The administrators had set a target of £500,000 to be raised to save the football club, with the local newspaper agreeing to match the amount raised by the trust. This work took Phillip all over his home city, where he met various people from diverse communities who came together for a common cause: to save the football club. Phillip was amazed by people's generosity, fundraising and commitment to saving the club, and realized the power of having something in common. It is this deep-rooted passion for bringing people together for a common good that inspires him in his role as Executive Director for Workforce and Organizational Development.

For Phillip, there is something special about his roots and where he comes from. Growing up, he had a keen interest in music, which he realizes had an influence on his values and mindset. He loved ska music, with The Specials being one of his favourite bands. The band were originally from Coventry, and the group was composed of black and white members, something that was rare at the time. The Specials were active in fighting against racism. There was a strange irony about this, as diverse and extreme political views were always held by those attending their concerts.

When it came to deciding on his career path, Phillip knew that he had a passion for working with people and development. He has always worked in workforce in the NHS and has a keen commitment to seeing people grow. In 2016, he presented to Health Education England about the high vacancy rate (12%) for registered nurses in the trust he worked with at the time, highlighting the lack of national and regional future workforce supply and the challenge of meeting the demand of future workforce supply. A week later, Phillip was contacted by a director of international health at Health Education England, who asked if Phillip would visit Hyderabad to partake in the Global Exchange Programme. This exchange programme was designed to bring 25,000 nurses to the UK to work on the 'Earn, Learn and Return' recruitment programme (NHS, 2023). This seemed like an ethical recruitment approach to Phillip. Nurses would be hired to work in the UK, be provided with opportunities to develop their skills whilst earning and then return to further health developments in their home countries.

Phillip had never been to Hyderabad before and describes the strange feeling of being the only white person during the time he was there. The feeling was not that different to what some ethnic minority colleagues experience in the NHS, giving him an appreciation of what it may feel like to be of ethnic minority background in the UK. He empathized with how international recruits must feel when they leave their family and give up their way of life to come and work for the NHS. Going to the school of nursing in Hyderabad was inspiring for Phillip, and it led to him putting forward his trust to take part in the recruitment programme on his return to the UK.

Following his visit, Phillip had a deeper appreciation of the challenges associated with moving to a new country. He therefore doubled his efforts to provide pastoral care for international recruits so that when they arrived, they had a community to be a part of and were able to access support.

Phillip enjoys working with people, and he volunteers with an organization called Across in his own time. This experience provides meaningful interactions with people who are sometimes nearing the end of life or have significant health conditions, encouraging Phillip to reflect on improvements that can be made in the workplace, such as reasonable adjustments for employees, and the patient experience. Volunteering helps shape Phillip's leadership style and how he chooses to lead, thereby shaping his values and behaviours.

Along the way, other people have joined Phillip's journey who have been instrumental in supporting race equality and putting in measures to support colleagues. One brought in a book called *Why Forgive?* (Arnold, 2014) for Phillip, and experiences like this have shaped him as a leader. This inspires him to develop other allies, and so he bought all the executives he works with two books: one about allyship, and another one called *Kinder Conversations* (Keogh, 2022). Phillip is driven by making a difference to the experience of the workforce and he sees it as a privilege to be able to serve others. This also means he finds it difficult when he hears of people's bad experiences in the trust. Not all of the 10,000 people in the trust that he leads are going to have had positive experiences.

I asked Phillip how he deals with it when things go wrong. He said he makes himself visible and makes the time and effort to go and speak to people across the organization. For example, when he is on call, he will visit ward areas. Sometimes this can be difficult, as he is an introvert, but he pushes himself out of his comfort zone and introduces himself to people, saying hello and asking how they are. Talking to people you don't know can sometimes be challenging for introverts, but as a leader, it is important to do so to connect with others and understand their experiences. During Black History Month, the REN arranged a cultural event where colleagues wore cultural dress and held a performance. After the event, Phillip heard their experiences over lunch, using the opportunity to listen. He noticed that one international nurse colleague was rather quiet, and he asked her how she was, where she worked and what her experience was like. He noticed the colleague's hesitation to respond and that she was upset about where she worked. Phillip felt he had to do something, as what you walk past is what you condone. Afterwards, he made the effort to speak with colleagues who would be able to support her. This is an example of how he leads by making a difference: he empowers others to be able to support the change he wishes to see.

He enjoys engaging with people, finding that he notices a lot more by engaging with the workforce, which supports him in understanding where there may be challenges, such as poorer staff experiences. Phillip also keeps a close eye on his priorities; for example, spending a day analysing reports on WRES and Workforce Disability Equality Standard (WDES) data so that he has a good understanding of what is happening within the trust and what measures are being taken to improve. He ensures that key performance indicator (KPI) targets are stretched to achieve the best progress, for example, maximizing the number of ethnic minority people in band 8c, 8a and 7 roles, because these are the breakthrough roles in aspiring for executive roles. Listening to lived experience alongside the governance and documentation feeds into feedback for the board on how the trust is doing, as well as giving an appreciation of how the workforce is being managed. Previously, people with disabilities were less likely to apply for jobs. In a short space of time, the number of people with a disability applying for jobs has risen to match the number of people who do not have a disability. However, for the WRES, the trust has still not yet achieved parity, which Phillip is keen to continue working on. To benchmark the trust's performance, he uses Model Hospital data to interrogate the causes of disparity and has a plan to address these through comprehensive action plans.

Phillip decided to volunteer for reciprocal mentoring. He has always been a mentor in various capacities, including having mentored HR professionals, CEOs and colleagues on leadership programmes. He had no expectations of being matched with someone but he had a match with a colleague of ethnic minority background. After their introduction, they realized that they were both from the same city and decided to meet in a local coffee shop – an informal space but one where they both felt comfortable and able to share their experiences. Phillip and his mentor built a positive relationship – to the point that they were supposed to meet for one hour one day but stayed for three hours. Phillip describes the relationship as very positive and says that he has learned a lot from his mentor, as well as sharing his own experiences and insight from his career. Phillip was keen to hear about the lived experience of his mentor and asked curious questions to understand her experiences and to further his cultural competency for making decisions in the organization. He recalls once asking for her input on hyper-local recruitment to ensure a diverse recruitment drive, giving her a leaflet and asking if she would kindly review it. She returned it a few days later having red-penned it all and provided some honest, authentic opinions on what the trust could do to improve diversity when recruiting.

For Phillip, there is a joy in seeing people develop, and so when the reciprocal mentoring programme was introduced, he was keen to support and help. Phillip advised his mentoring partner on career options and what she could do to enhance her professional development. He describes how he genuinely looked forward to the mentoring meetings, because they developed him in a world where the workforce composition is changing. This enabled Phillip to be his authentic self, and a positive and equal relationship developed between the two individuals that did not differentiate between their levels in the organization of executive and junior colleague. It is important to be able to develop a meaningful relationship with a mentor that provides mutual benefit.

When reflecting on his role as a mentor, Phillip says he has played an instrumental role in supporting his colleagues. He acknowledges that it is not possible to help everyone through mentoring on an individual basis but that there is value in building close relationships with people through expanding one's networks and therefore opportunities. Ethnic minority individuals tend to find that we aren't given a space to be able to develop from networking opportunities, and I think some of this comes from the challenge around building the right relationships and is not necessarily reflective of ability or potential.

A shadow culture exists in the NHS that consciously or subconsciously excludes people of certain backgrounds and characteristics (Young, 2013). The opportunity to progress or develop is not always accessible, which is why initiatives like The Fellowship programme (see Chapter 11), reciprocal mentoring and specific leadership programmes provide an opportunity for people who are otherwise unseen or unheard to demonstrate their potential and thereby succeed. Provision of programmes that support development are essential. Development can be a challenge if there are not any programmes in place.

In 2018, Phillip's trust did not run or support the delivery of any leadership programmes for BAME staff. Phillip worked hard to change this, and four years later, the trust offered specific leadership programmes for under-represented groups and commenced its third successful cohort of reciprocal mentoring. The trust also boasted the highest number of applicants on the highly sought-after BAME fellowship programme mentioned earlier, which was run by the regional ICB. This change in career opportunities is testimony to how far the organization has come in developing and providing opportunities.

Phillip admits that he is not an expert on race equality and that there were times when it didn't work out as quickly as he wanted. One example was the RCN Cultural Ambassador Programme, which the trust agreed to support. This RCN initiative trained volunteers to support decision-making panels for investigations, grievances and disciplinary hearings where a BAME staff member was affected (Royal College of Nursing, 2023). The cultural ambassador role aims to identify and explore issues that may result in potential discrimination, cultural bias or being treated less favourably. Whilst cultural ambassadors may not have a direct role in influencing the outcome, their role is to be curious, honest and transparent in sharing their views and to create dialogues that establish the potential impact of the outcome so lessons can be learned. Whilst the trust funded and supported this programme, there has been slow development in implementing the cultural ambassadors effectively, and the programme finished three years ago. Phillip is keen to see a cultural ambassador as part of the interview panel at every senior appointment in the future, recognizing the commitment to the EDI agenda. Phillip has not lost sight of this work and continues to drive this with his senior leadership team.

His commitment to race equality as an executive director is demonstrated through the actions taken to improve staff experience and his vision and drive to improve racial equality. But there is sometimes a lack of this filtering down to those across the organization who are experiencing racism. Establishing staff networks has helped with this, as has inviting people to trust board seminars to share their lived experiences, which is both educational and thought-provoking. Also key to this work is using KPIs to provide practical, tangible measures to improve diversity at all levels and running recruitment days in the local area to ensure recruitment is taking place amongst local populations that the trust is there to serve. Phillip sees local recruitment as being key to improving health inequalities by providing a regular income to support financial wellbeing, improving access to education and tackling health inequalities through greater health awareness. For Phillip, the patient experience is as important as the staff experience, and everything that is done must be co-led, co-managed and co-created. The process takes time, and sometimes things may go wrong, but more important than this is how you learn from it.

Some aspects of Phillip's background – where and how he grew up, his personal experiences – have shaped how he operates, which could be a part of what drives his curiosity to understand the workforce and the differences in experiences that exist within it. While Phillip comes from Bradford, for a period he worked in Harrogate, and there are stark differences between the two places. Bradford has a high ethnic minority population with high deprivation levels, whereas Harrogate is a wealthy spa town, known for its elegant tea rooms and rolling countryside (Britannica, 2023). These differences mean that people's experiences of life, education, housing, wealth, etc. are going to be different. But for Phillip, curiosity is what helps him to understand and appreciate the similarities and differences that exist. The best way to understand people is to talk to them and learn from what they say.

After Phillip's experiences of reciprocal mentoring, he introduced an initiative whereby there are trust board champions for each of the protected characteristics. For example, the CEO is race champion, and Phillip is the champion for those who are married or in a civil partnership. There have been varying degrees of success with this initiative, which comes down to the commitment of the named champion to educate, inform and engage with people of the protected characteristic that they are championing.

Phillip has also experienced some criticism from colleagues in this space too. He shared a BAME leadership programme and was asked why there wasn't one for white staff. Phillip defended his position by highlighting the importance of positive action (UK Government, 2023). Positive action is outlined in the Equality Act 2010, which allows employers to take specific actions to overcome a disadvantage, have needs met or participate in a particular activity related to employment for those with protected characteristics. It is a proportionate way to enable groups who have protected characteristics to meet their employment needs. This is not to be confused with positive discrimination, which is considered unlawful. The difference between the two is that positive discrimination (otherwise known as unlawful direct discrimination) favours a particular group and does not meet the statutory requirements of the Equality Act 2010, whereas positive action aligns with the requirements outlined in the Act, as above. For Phillip, recognizing that the experiences of BAME people are worse than those of their white counterparts was a stimulating factor for implementing positive action. Sharing BAME leadership programmes was therefore an act of positive action, as was running a leadership programme of the same category that was available for all staff.

Allyship and Covid-19

As a senior leader in the space of allyship, the Covid-19 pandemic was a very challenging period for Phillip. The role became very different, posing significant challenges that had not been seen before. He remembers 440,000 lateral flow tests being delivered to the trust and being responsible for delivering a testing approach within a week. He led the work to establish a drive-through testing centre, managing increasing absences and workforce availability. Elective services were stopped, and people were redeployed in acute areas. Having enough PPE to protect staff when supplies were short was a worry. There were daily command and control meetings to discuss the ever-evolving situation. There were early indicators of the impact of Covid-19 on ethnic minority groups, and Phillip worked closely with the EDI lead to develop risk assessments to support staff. The trust lost an Asian colleague to Covid-19 early on, and Phillip liaised with the family to support them through that time. Despite being a constantly evolving and challenging period, the pandemic strengthened Phillip's values of helping others. When colleagues contracted the virus and were unwell, Phillip made the time and space to check how they were doing to ensure they were being supported during that time. For Phillip, compassion and care is important, whether it's for the one person on the intensive care unit (ICU) or the 9000 other employees.

Phillip led BAME webinars for staff who needed a safe space to communicate how they felt and raise their concerns. Mistakes were sometimes made, and it was a time when the stark under-representation of BAME people was of concern. Allyship was key, given the concerns for BAME colleagues, who noticed that most of the patients who were seriously unwell with Covid-19 seemed to be of ethnic minority background. Phillip strengthened his role as an ally during this time.

When asked about his advice for other allies, he suggests immersing yourself in listening to other people and their experiences, because it makes you a far better leader than any theoretical programme of study you could ever undertake. People don't leave the NHS, they leave bad teams and managers, and this comes down to the core basics of working conditions: are you having team briefs, is your job description up to date, are you having regular one-to-ones, do you feel valued?

As a director, Phillip regularly sends cards of appreciation to people across the trust. He purchased 15 copies of Tim Keogh's book, *Kinder Conversations*, and distributed it to executives across the trust. In the book, there is a simple model called ABC, which is about appreciation of others (Keogh, 2022). It is based on the principles of: A) Action, B) Behaviour and C) Continue. The model aims to show

how people can be appreciative of positive behaviours exhibited by others, which supports success in the workplace by building better positive relationships as opposed to using critical feedback. Phillip asked the communications team to design a small card with the model on that could be issued. The second model Phillip uses is the BUILD model: 'behaviour; understand the impact and learning, and continue to develop', as taught in the 'A Kind Life' teaching from Tim Keogh, the author of *Kinder Conversations*. This is a simple method for showing kindness in an organization, which is the culture that Phillip strives to develop – whilst being accountable for what we are here to deliver and do.

Phillip's advice to BAME colleagues would be to seize every opportunity that presents itself. Join networks and actively take part in them. Be vocal at work and bring your whole self to work. Push the boundaries and speak up when things aren't right. Live to the values of the organization. Familiarize yourself with the routes for progression and take active steps towards achieving it. When it comes to striving to improve race equality, Phillip suggests reviewing the regional average and comparing this with representation reflected in each of the bands across the organization. He suggests asking whether it is reflective of the local population. Equity is representation right through the organization, and if that isn't there, ask why. Hold listening events, monitor satisfaction scores and where the differences lie, and implement reciprocal mentoring schemes to develop cultural competency, learning from the experiences of others in the process.

To be a leader in the NHS means you need to understand how different people work, as well as their values, culture and identities, because it is your role to represent everyone. If you don't, how are you doing your best by the people you are here to serve? Attending staff networks and listening to staff perspectives is a good start. Working closely with EDI leads can help, despite the recent controversy mentioned in Chapter 5 following ex-Secretary of State for Health and Social Care Steve Barclay's letter asking leaders to remove NHS EDI roles (Taylor, Mortimer and Walter, 2023). Following this letter, Phillip immediately spoke to his EDI team to assure them that no redundancies would be made and he further asked the communications team to highlight the value of the EDI team publicly.

Roles like this when they are performed well provide the equity that trusts need in terms of staff and patient experience. Without them, who would do the work for the WRES and WDES or report to trust committees for this agenda? Who would help in the programmes driving inclusion and review the services to ensure they serve the communities amongst the population? Several employers, senior leaders and NHS organizations, including the NHS Confederation, NHS Providers, *Nursing Times* and *The BMJ*, wrote letters in response to Steve Barclay's letter, rejecting his surmise that EDI roles do not provide purpose or value for money (Faragher, 2023). Going forward, Phillip plans to continue to work closely alongside his EDI colleagues and is keen to see and deliver the change he desires in improving ethnic minority representation, eliminating discrimination and providing equitable career opportunities for all.

> **Reflective questions**
>
> * Have you signed up to reciprocal mentoring? Is it something that you could look at initiating in your organization?
> * What three steps could you take to demonstrate allyship, whether personally or publicly?
> * Is there anyone in your organization who could support you on this journey? Could reaching out to the EDI team help?

— CHAPTER 10 —

Allyship Case Study 2: An Ally's Experience

As we continue to explore allyship, this chapter will discuss:

- an ally's experience of observing racial inequalities
- what Renee* feels she can do as a white ally
- barriers to allyship.

Allyship helps to raise awareness about racial inequalities and, more importantly, supports doing something about it. Change takes time, but the more people are involved and supportive, the quicker progress is made and the more meaningful it is. Allyship comes in various forms and can apply to anyone regardless of role, position or race. Some people are confident in speaking about race equality and its importance, whereas others know racism is wrong but are not quite sure what to do about it. Others observe it but do not feel confident speaking up or know what to do to support others. Whilst they do not consider themselves allies, they are not sure what the word means and whether it applies to them. However, their actions and support align with allyship, and they believe in standing up for others when they are being treated unfairly.

I spoke with Renee, an AHP who works in a mental health trust in the north of England. Renee has worked in the NHS for over 30 years and has seen various changes in management, service delivery and patient demographics over the years. As mentioned earlier, black patients are significantly over-represented in mental health settings, and they are more likely to be detained and sectioned. Whilst it would not be correct to say that this is solely due to racism, it is difficult to deny that structural factors embedding racism within wider society play a part in the over-representation of black people in mental health settings.

Renee does not see herself as an ally, as she says she 'does not do very much'. She says she comes from a very 'white background' – the county town of Rutland, hailed as the smallest county town in England, in the East Midlands. She left school in the 1980s, having not had a great education but wanting to do something with her life. She tried various roles and then fell into a care role, which she thoroughly enjoyed and that led to her passion for nursing. The experience of working in different roles helped her to understand what she liked to do, standing her in good stead to begin her career in her chosen field.

After leaving Rutland, she moved to Leeds, living in Chapeltown. Leeds is a large, diverse city and Chapeltown is a multicultural area, which is the opposite of Rutland. It was a surprise for Renee to see people of diverse backgrounds, as this was very different from where she grew up. However, she enjoyed it and found herself making good friends amongst a range of people in her local area.

As she continued her career, she worked in different healthcare settings. The first ward she worked on, in 1992, was in a mental health institution. She describes herself as a naïve student, soaking up the new experience of working as a healthcare professional. She made the stark observation that those who were sectioned in the secure unit tended to be black men, which she found quite surprising. She describes them as generally being taller and more expressive but not necessarily aggressive – as the media would sometimes describe them. In Renee's experience, black men were more likely to be using mental health services. Over 30 years later, recent research shows that black people are still more likely to experience common mental health conditions, being 27 per cent more likely to be in contact with mental health services than their white counterparts (Baker and Kirk-Wade, 2023). Black or black British people are over four times more likely to be detained than their white counterparts (NHS Digital, 2017). These are shocking figures, considering that black people make up less than 20 per cent of the UK population.

It is concerning that there has been little change in the over-representation of black people in mental health services over this 30-year period. In fact, this issue first came to light in the 1970s, and there has been little change since then. But why is this the case? What is causing this increase in mental health disorders amongst black people in the UK, when these levels of mental health issues are not seen in African or Caribbean countries with larger populations of black people? Qassem *et al.* (2015) say the social and economic disadvantages that black people are more likely to experience are a significant factor, and institutional racism plays a part in this. If a person is viewed suspiciously by the system, their cultural differences are not considered or their identity is 'othered', they are not going to feel like it is a space where they are able to be their whole selves, which can lead to issues with mental health, confidence and self-esteem. From an NHS perspective, we need to ask how we are ensuring that this isn't the case, when our constitution states:

> [The NHS] has a wider social duty to promote equality through the services it provides and to pay particular attention to groups or sections of society where improvements in health and life expectancy are not keeping pace with the rest of the population. (Department of Health and Social Care, 2023)

In Renee's experience, structural racism contributes to people of ethnic minority background in the UK being failed. When she noticed the over-representation of black people in mental health settings, she felt it was wrong, but being young and inexperienced, she did not know what to do about it. She describes herself as being a shy person, so speaking up felt difficult. Many years later, as an experienced professional, her confidence to speak up for what she feels is right has grown. There was a time when she did not have the confidence to speak up, which can be common. People fear the consequences of speaking up, even when it is right, such as a backlash, being scapegoated or re-experiencing previous negative consequences. The 2022 NHS Staff Survey highlighted that 38.5 per cent of employees feel unable to speak up about their concerns, and the figure was higher amongst people of ethnic minority background, people with long-term conditions and bank/agency workers (Chidgey-Clark, 2023). Less than half (48.7%) of employees felt confident that their concerns would be addressed.

Despite the investment in Freedom to Speak Up Guardians and encouraging people to raise concerns, a fear of speaking up remains, particularly when it comes to topics deemed 'sensitive' or 'controversial', and race equality can sometimes be portrayed in this way. Leaders should take an active role in understanding what stops people from speaking up. When concerns are raised, they should be sure to address these sensitively and appropriately. Organizations have a responsibility to embed a culture that supports people to speak up and actively addresses concerns raised, which contributes to better patient safety and care, as well as an environment in which people are happier to work. Resolving racial inequality will likely positively impact poor recruitment and retention rates, as people feel valued and are more likely to stay with an employer when they are respected and treated well.

The hierarchical nature of the NHS can result in it being challenging to influence cultures that embed racial inequalities. Renee recalls a time when she was working on the wards. She had a patient who'd had bowel issues after taking antibiotics and therefore needed to have live yoghurt as part of her treatment. The ward sister took the approach that the patient could not have a dessert because she needed to have the yoghurt, so the patient was not allowed to have dessert. In fact, there was no restriction on the patient having dessert; this was just the sister's interpretation. One day, the sister was not on the ward, and Renee said that the patient could have the yoghurt later and choose a dessert if she wanted. The patient was ecstatic that she could have a dessert, but as Renee approached her with the dessert in her hand, the patient caught her eye and told her 'no' as she looked behind Renee. The sister was standing behind Renee but Renee said the patient could have the dessert anyway. However, the patient was so fearful of what the sister would say that she declined the dessert. This caused some conflict between Renee and the sister, and was one of Renee's first experiences in speaking up. Speaking up can be difficult, and people are less likely to do it if the wider support isn't there.

As Renee continued to speak up about situations regarding patient safety, she felt targeted for doing so. Renee describes it as a challenging period but says that with her (in her words) 'white privilege', she had it easier than some. She describes policies that were implemented but seemed meaningless and guardians who were recruited to manage issues but didn't do so effectively. This paints a bleak picture of working in an environment where people do not have the confidence to raise their concerns. Renee's advice for this sort of situation is to be alert. There are, of course, benefits in working for the NHS: it is a rewarding role and provides job security, pensions, benefits and the pride that comes with public service. But there is still a long way to go in providing an equitable space for colleagues. When working within the system, it can be easier to support or deliver change. When working outside of the system, it can often be harder to influence. When challenging the system to be the change you want to see, it is easy to burn out. It is therefore important to look after yourself. Some people can take a break or take time to recover from burnout, but some can't do this. Perhaps they have bills to pay or a family to feed and are reliant on an income. In these cases, the fear about speaking up can feel greater, leaving people feeling quiet and discontent, and they may eventually resign or take extended sick leave to recover from poor mental health and wellbeing because of a situation they feel unable to raise their concerns about.

As Renee observed the racial dynamics within her workplace, she noticed that the care support workers and lower bands tended to be a mix of ethnic backgrounds. Those in band 6 and above were all white and nearly all male, with the rare exception of a female. It seemed to be a pattern within mental health settings, and she noticed it throughout her career, even in different settings. She noticed it even more when she became a band 6 and attended senior meetings.

Over the last six years, she has observed that there are now more doctors who are black. There is a high proportion of doctors of BAME background, whose journeys to becoming consultants are marred with racism. Racism hinders their career progression and results in lower pay and worse working conditions compared with their white counterparts (Gregory, 2022). The British Medical Association reports that this difference in treatment by the system is what leads to BAME doctors leaving the NHS, with 42 per cent of black and 41 per cent of Asian doctors considering leaving or having already left (BMA, 2022). Considering the struggles to retain and recruit staff to manage and deliver services, this is alarming. Long-term consequences of this situation include the limited sustainability of the healthcare system and the impact on those experiencing racism who are unable to practise their profession.

They choose to leave to protect their own wellbeing, employment prospects and mental health, which the employer has failed to do. This must be a difficult decision to make, especially after spending so much time, effort and money on training in a demanding role, and doctors should not be viewed negatively for taking the decision to protect their own wellbeing. Rather, the role of the employer in failing to protect them should be reviewed.

BAME health professionals earn 6.3 per cent less than their white counterparts on average, with variance amongst different levels (e.g., doctors, support workers, management) ranging from 2.3 per cent to 14 per cent (Moberly, 2018). Additionally, whilst doctors may have autonomy over clinical treatment, assessment and accountability for an aspect of clinical care and service delivery, management very rarely has any level of diverse representation. Management structures generally control the decisions of spending, influence, grievances, investigations, annual leave and study entitlement, all of which support the running of an effective service and looking after staff. If the working relationship between management and the team (or staff) is marred with racism and bullying, this will impact how well a doctor can perform or feels supported in the workplace.

Renee wanted to understand her BAME colleagues' experiences in the workplace and what she could do about it, so she decided to attend an REN meeting. She was dumbfounded to hear colleagues describe the racism they had experienced from staff. Whilst she was aware that racism exists, she was shocked that people in her professional place of work had the brazenness to feel that they could be racist in the workplace with no repercussions. On the other side, we have BAME colleagues who are afraid of bringing their whole selves to work and rarely experience a sense of belonging (NHS England, 2020). Colleagues describe feeling that they cannot be their 'true' selves at work and feeling the need to hide their identity to avoid being bullied or targeted because of their background. Renee worked with a doctor of ethnic minority background who was a reserved person and did not engage in much conversation with colleagues unless it was clinically necessary. No one knew his ethnicity, but eventually, over time, he built a relationship with his colleagues, and years later he felt confident to disclose his ethnicity. He was from Iraq, and world events at the time (around when the 9/11 attack happened) meant that he felt he could not express who he truly was out of fear of being targeted or treated differently.

Renee recalls a doctor of Chinese background casually telling her about a time when she was walking down the street and someone shouted, 'Go back home,' at her. Renee was appalled to hear this, but her colleague said that it happened a lot less there than down south. One does wonder where such brazenness in racist behaviour comes from, but the reality is that we do not work and live in a vacuum. The racism often observed in the NHS is reflective of what we see across society. Being exposed to such behaviour can affect an individual's confidence and self-esteem. If managers do not provide support through such situations, this can lead to disengagement and low morale.

Additionally, if someone does not feel a sense of belonging where they work, they may not feel comfortable expressing their full identity or even ethnicity. Information on ethnicity within the NHS has been notoriously limited, often due to poor data collection. Renee's trust does not do well in its collecting of minimum datasets that include information on ethnicity. In the 1990s, a patient's ethnicity was assumed by the professional, and patients were not necessarily asked about it. Sometimes it wouldn't even be recorded at all. It is not always appropriate to ask about someone's ethnicity in a crisis or acute situation where the priority is the treatment and access to care. But this data matters from a data collection perspective, so it should be collected at some point during a patient's care. Without data, we cannot understand the differences in care, the accessibility of services and whether there is equity in the services provided. Prior to the introduction of the WRES, the needs of ethnic minority patients and staff were little understood because there was no data to understand their experiences and no measures to evaluate key impacts.

Quantitative data can be gathered through data collection methods, but qualitative data can be gathered through listening to people's experiences. To better understand lived experiences, Renee tries to stimulate conversations about race at work. As a white person, she describes feeling guilt about the fact that there is not equality in the way that people of different backgrounds are treated. When she grew up in the 1970s, comedians would regularly make racist jokes. It was common to see signs reading, 'No blacks, no Irish, no dogs,' to prevent certain people from entering public spaces. Whilst in one sense we have come a long way, racism has become more hidden instead of being overt. Race relations have been improved to some extent by the introduction of legislation such as the Equality Act 2010, hate crimes becoming a punishable offence by law and the work done to encourage intercommunity relationships. But this has also pushed some of the racism underground, as people are aware of the repercussions of exhibiting such behaviour, therefore become subtler in the ways in which they express it.

Given that racism is a societal issue, I asked Renee whether it was fair to blame the healthcare system for the prevalence of racism in the NHS and she said yes. Healthcare is a professional, caring institution mandated to look after everybody, but we still see variances in treatment that have been documented for many years and have changed very little. There must be some accountability for allowing racism to continue when we know that it has existed in the past and continues to do so now. Whilst you can't stop racist people working for the NHS, the system can work to disempower them. You can support those affected by it, you can learn to change your approach and you can reflect on your power and giving it up or using it to ensure equity. But this requires a willingness to do so, which is where leaders can fall short and where allies should take the lead, particularly those who hold power and are able to influence decisions.

What does white power look like? It is the space you occupy because you have had the privileges, the support network, the 'helping hand' that others did not. It's not being looked at because of your accent, or the colour of your skin, or your religious beliefs. It's about people seeing what you do, not what you are. You can't give up the privilege that got you where you are, but you can hold that space open for others and invite them to be a part of it. This occurs at different levels and depends on everyone's role and circumstances. Pushing yourself out of your comfort zone to challenge racist behaviour matters. Attending cultural competency training to understand other cultures and beliefs matters. And having an openness and vulnerability with people that invites them to be open with you matters too.

Renee and I discussed whether British culture supports this approach. Renee thinks that the rise of increasingly right-wing rhetoric means it does not. While we previously prided ourselves on fairness and being open and tolerant, this is changing due to our controversial immigration schemes and the rhetoric used to describe people of different nationalities who are fleeing persecution or war (Syal and Taylor, 2023). This is despite the Rwanda scheme being ruled unlawful by the UK Supreme Court on the grounds of the risk of asylum seekers being sent back to the countries they are fleeing, as well as referencing similar failed schemes between Israel and Rwanda. This was rightly met with concern by various bodies including the UN, human rights organizations, human rights and immigration lawyers, and various charities supporting asylum seekers. For those of immigrant or refugee backgrounds who are living in the UK, this paints an unwelcoming picture, and this rhetoric contributes to a rise in hate crime, as seen in the targeting of asylum processing centres such as the attacks in Knowsley, Merseyside (Jackson, 2023).

Amongst increasing hateful rhetoric towards diverse communities, isolation and loneliness are on the rise in the UK, with 3.7 million adults feeling lonely (Siddique, 2021). This leads to communities breaking down because we 'other' people and create divisions rather than appreciating others. Brexit no doubt played a part in this, with the UK witnessing a 25 per cent increase in hate crime following the divisive vote to leave the European Union (Carr *et al.*, 2021). The prevalence of societal racism contributes to institutional racism within the very systems that make up society – societal and institutional racism do not exist in separate vacuums. This does not absolve institutions of responsibility when tackling issues like widespread racism – the change must start somewhere. You can't expect people to provide person-centred care if you are not providing a person-centred work environment. If you don't develop, support and provide opportunities for staff, how will they empower others to do the same? How will they empower patients to manage their health if they don't feel empowered themselves?

We discussed the future of the NHS, and Renee suspects it will continue to fragment under the pressures of too much demand, not enough funding and a workforce we are struggling to retain. This could push back the race equality agenda due to conflicting acute priorities. When training and development of services is cancelled to accommodate service demand, employees then do not have the time to consider other priorities when working in clinical environments. Whilst patient care obviously takes precedence, prioritizing it in a constant firefighting state leads to burnout, stress and low morale. It doesn't support the wider system in supporting its workforce. Renee recalls talking to a social worker who described how every assignment and piece of work for her degree had to include information on how they would be anti-racist. This is an interesting concept, and it has not yet been seen across other healthcare education courses. It would likely be powerful if it were implemented and more importantly, practised. It may also encourage consideration of wider perspectives, leading to better holistic care that considers broader factors that affect the healthcare of patients.

It can be difficult to demonstrate to Gen Z why they would want to work for an employer that hasn't been able to tackle decades of institutional racism and be underpaid and overworked. In an era where influencing is considered a top career choice, work–life balance is more valued than overworking. If there is a preference for roles that stimulate creativity and innovation, what does the NHS offer? Generally, those of us who work in healthcare enter the system because we have a passion for helping others. We do so because the human body and mind are fascinating, and working in healthcare provides an opportunity to develop, discover and learn remarkable things about the human body and its function. It is a place where we support people in their most vulnerable moments, helping them with recovery and function, and making the transition from life to death easier when medicine can no longer make a difference. And it amazes me that the NHS still has issues with racism when its foundations were built on being compassionate and caring for others.

We have serious work to do in terms of providing attractive recruitment opportunities, and this begins with ensuring that there is a culture where everyone feels a sense of belonging. That starts with eliminating systemic racism, and all allies, whether aspiring or established, have a part to play in making sure everyone feels they can bring their full self to work.

Reflective questions

* Would you be confident to address race equality in your workplace? Reflect on why you feel this way.

* Have you witnessed racist behaviour in your workplace? What would you do in future if it were to arise again?

* What actions could you take to become an ally in your circle of influence?

* Do you feel confident in bringing your whole identity to work? If not, what would feeling confident about bringing your whole self to work look like for you? Are there steps you can take to feel confident in doing so?

— CHAPTER 11 —

Allyship Case Study 3: Accomplished Ally

This chapter will discuss:

- the role of NHS West Yorkshire Integrated Care Board (ICB) and Integrated Care System (ICS) in delivering health and care
- race inequalities
- leadership and race equality
- what RENs do.

This case study examines the role that leaders play in addressing racial inequalities, and how Rob Webster set out to address them in his role as Chief Executive of the NHS West Yorkshire ICB, which is part of West Yorkshire Health and Care Partnership, an ICS.

West Yorkshire ICS serves a population of 2.4 million people (West Yorkshire Health and Care Partnership, 2023a). Around 490,000 people are from a minority community background, making up 20 per cent of the population. Having worked in the health and care system for 30 years, Rob is experienced in and known for his social justice values and practical-actions approach.

As Chief Executive of the NHS West Yorkshire ICB, Rob wants it to be a place where everyone in the area has the best possible health and wellbeing outcomes so they have every chance of living a long and healthy life. Having a strong focus on tackling the determinants of health inequalities for everyone – particularly those with protected characteristics – makes a difference not only in how health is accessed but also in how people interact with the ICS. To understand the next case study, it is important to comprehend the context of how care is delivered across the NHS, and what roles ICBs and ICSs play.

Previously, NHS trusts received money to deliver services from bodies known as Strategic Health Authorities (Edwards and Buckingham, 2020). These were replaced with Clinical Commissioning Groups (CCGs), which provided payment for the delivery of services based on the previous year's activity (NHS Confederation, 2021) and the size of the population being served in the local area. CCGs were disbanded in July 2022 and ICBs were formed. The role of the ICS is to support this approach, as laid out by law in the Health and Care Act 2022, to fund place-based care and encourage any health and wellbeing organizations at 'place' level to work together to provide care (Charles, 2020).

The ICS consists of NHS organizations, councils, Healthwatch, hospices, social enterprises, charities, the community and voluntary organizations. For example, across all the places in West Yorkshire, including Leeds, NHS organizations, the local city council, charity organizations and social enterprises find ways to work together to deliver better health and care for people in the area. The West Yorkshire Health and Care Partnership employs over 100,000 colleagues in total (this does not include private providers of social care or the thousands of volunteers working in local communities).

For many years, healthcare was delivered based on episodic care, which treated the problems that patients came in with. For example, Mr Smith with a back injury would go to his GP, be referred to the hospital, treated for his pain and then sent back home again. His previous healthcare history or occupation may be given some consideration, but little would impact how his care would be delivered and the factors that led to him needing to come to hospital. The issue with this type of delivery of care is that wider healthcare determinants are ignored, and there is a failure to understand why people experience illness, particularly when deterioration in health is preventable. Additionally, not every illness is curable and so it is important to see the person holistically instead of focusing on their presenting health condition. Conditions like obesity, diabetes and cancer have a much higher prevalence in communities that are poorer or less able or likely to access healthcare (Williams *et al.,* 2022). It is therefore not enough to treat the problems that people present with; it's also crucial to understand the person and the root cause of the issues that are impacting their health and wellbeing in order to develop a preventative approach. Reviewing how and why people experience illness shows that factors outside of the NHS play a part in health and wellbeing. Where you live, your job and your access to education, healthcare and green spaces all play a part in how well you live. Or, as Rob puts it, 'We all need somewhere to live, someone to love and something to do.'

When asked about the factors that affect the usability of healthcare, Rob says he believes that around 10 per cent of the issues with healthcare are due to access and whether people know how to get the help, care and support they need, and 10 per cent are down to the quality of care and whether it meets their expectations. Managing problems with a mindset that understands the role of varying factors in healthcare helps to identify the root cause, with a view to then solving this. The rest of the issues with healthcare are about varying complexities, which is where local authorities, charities, communities and public health have a role. The BMA identified three main areas that would improve the worsening ill health of the UK: economic security so people can afford a healthy life; public services that are properly funded; the introduction and maintenance of policies that support good public health (BMA, 2022). All were deemed to be determinants in improving the health and wellbeing of people in the UK.

Most of the places within West Yorkshire – Bradford District and Craven, Calderdale, Kirklees, Leeds, and Wakefield District – have different health and wellbeing outcomes, including the stark differences in life expectancy. Across Leeds, the average life expectancy is 80 years; however, people in more affluent areas of the city can expect to live up to 12 years longer than those living in deprived areas (Centre for Ageing Better, 2021). The mortality rate for females living in deprived areas is 40 per cent higher than it is for their counterparts living in wealthier areas (White, Erskine and Seims, 2019). In Wakefield, there is a similar pattern of inequalities in life expectancy between the most deprived areas and the least deprived areas, with a difference in life expectancy of 9.2 years for males and 8.2 years for females (Office for National Statistics, 2021). When reviewing what factors impact this, different experiences and outcomes are described by people with protected characteristics, including (but not limited to) disability, age and race, with race being one of the major areas where negative differences in experience and health outcomes are widely and consistently reported (Magadi and Magadi, 2022).

Tackling race inequalities as a leader

Rob reflected on his first conversation, over 20 years ago, about the differences in experience of those who access care, namely between people from minority communities and white people. I asked Rob whether it was a surprise to hear about these differences, and he said that it wasn't. Having been the leader of the ICS since 2016, Rob decided to review the areas where inequalities existed by having an honest conversation about what the inequalities meant for people. For example, people who have a learning disability and are of minority ethnic background are more likely to die 26 years earlier than their counterparts who do not have a disability and are of white background (Umpleby et al., 2023). While this isn't a surprise, it is still shocking. When it came to reviewing racial inequalities, Rob found that the experience of both BAME employees and BAME people who accessed care was generally poorer than that of the rest of the population, but at the time there was little data as to why this disparity existed. During this period, Rob was CEO of a mental health trust and was keen to hear about the lived experiences of people who worked in the trust to better understand what could be done to improve existing disparities.

Rob firmly believes that significant leadership talent exists within West Yorkshire but inequalities hold people back from achieving career progression and opportunities. After meeting with a colleague and hearing about their experiences, he made a note of the BAME networks and ensured that the people who wanted to set up and lead staff networks were supported to do so. The executive directors were also keen to ensure that this was led by individual staff members who could own the agenda and be supported in doing so.

When Rob moved on to the post of CEO lead of the ICS, he was aware that there was not much diversity amongst the board. There were strong champions, but it was important to have lived experiences and representation at decision-making levels. To tackle this,

Rob supported the West Yorkshire Race Equality Network development, which went on to develop various initiatives for colleagues across the area, including commissioning the independent race review in 2020 and implementing the Health Inequality Academy and Fellowship Leadership Programme. Rob's response to racial inequalities was guided by a combination of experience and analysis. In his first CEO role in the NHS, he was fortunate to work with other CEOs who were keen to understand the experience of people of different communities in the NHS. BAME people were more likely to say that they had fewer career opportunities, more likely to be bullied and more likely to be harassed in their workplace, which was astonishing but not unexpected. Driven by his values of social justice, Rob reviewed the key issues leading to such experiences and had the tenacity to not shy away from addressing difficult issues.

It is important to note the power of leadership and values. Rob's values include ambition, openness and transparency, all of which drive the work he wishes to achieve. He is keen for leaders to relay to others what they wish to achieve and define their narrative clearly. This encourages them to reflect on 'why' they do what they do. Does personal or political gain hold more interest than making a positive difference to people's lives in whatever way you can? Rob focuses on people's potential and the outcomes for communities, and he balances his work with politicians and communities.

Rob wants the system to be open and transparent when making decisions. He wants good governance and decision-making, with people's voices at the heart of everything the ICS and ICB do and leadership at every level. He strives for vibrant energy and efficiency to do as much as possible to empower staff and communities to make decisions. This leads to the creation of community leaders who strive collectively and work towards a common goal. The common goal comes from establishing the same or a similar set of values that are focused on improving outcomes for people in the region, as they all live and work there and want it to be better.

As a trust leader, Rob worked with the REN as it went through a process of reimagining itself. Rob describes a great colleague who was keen to empower staff to reshape the network as they wished to see it rather than how the organization wanted it to be. It took a long time to develop, but once it came to fruition, staff owned the network, which brought people together and gained influence and advocacy for ethnic minority colleagues across the trust.

The network invited the executive team to an event where lived experiences were shared. This experience taught Rob the importance of supporting equity, the value of reciprocal mentoring and the power of having a similar and shared set of values with the people he worked alongside. Rob brought this approach to the ICS and ICB. The West Yorkshire Health and Care Partnership is recognized nationally for its willingness to challenge itself and be visible about what it does, which has been tough at times due to the constructive criticism it invites, which can be hard to hear. Nevertheless, this level of engagement and inclusion led to it acting to instigate change after hearing about people's lived experiences.

As the ICS lead, Rob had a chance conversation with a colleague from a minority community background who described his experience of working in healthcare. The colleague said that the main issue was the challenge of the under-representation of certain groups of people across the West Yorkshire health and care system. They both agreed to present to the System Leadership Executive Group (SLEG). This was an important and influential group consisting of CEOs from across West Yorkshire organizations – council CEOs, trust chiefs and care provider chiefs – and the topic of under-representation of colleagues from minority communities in West Yorkshire had been tabled for the next meeting. Rob asked a group of people to design a session that asked a range of people – from CEOs to junior staff – challenging questions, for example, 'Why do I need extra training?' 'Why do people from minority groups get preferential treatment?' These were difficult questions to ask, and we still see this narrative peddled in parts of the UK today, but asking them is necessary for having honest dialogue and understanding how such racial inequalities arise.

The role of the ICS in tackling race inequalities

The aim of the meeting was to stimulate honest conversations about the real experiences of people in the organizations and encourage partnership leaders to reflect on the issues raised. From this came a sense of taking action to improve the experiences of everyone across West Yorkshire. One of the actions from this meeting was to be honest about the RENs in each organization across the area – were these well functioning, supported by leaders in organizations and making a difference? And were the people whom they needed to serve feeling supported?

BAME network leaders narrated mixed experiences, with some reporting that they were included at board meetings, felt supported by the board and felt supported to make a difference in their organization. Others reported that nobody in their organization cared, they felt like it was a struggle to manage and they did not feel empowered to make the differences they wished to see. The CEOs were listening, and they agreed that the space was necessary to create support for the networks to develop. The senior leadership of the executive group agreed to recognize under-representation of colleagues as a strategic priority and commissioned work to support leaders and networks to improve representation. As actions finally began to be taken, the Covid-19 pandemic struck, which had a disproportionate impact on minority communities, as highlighted by Public Health England (2020). West Yorkshire ICS recognized that there was little representation of diverse communities around the decision-making table to put forward their views and share their needs.

Rob worked closely with Sam Allen (Chief Executive of the Northeast and North Cumbria ICS) to highlight the importance of representative leadership through targeted efforts. Rob brought in colleagues to the ICS who were able to represent different communities. Colleagues already in strategic roles who were keen to progress to board roles were invited to offer their advice and insight at the leadership table. Not all ICSs have such systems to provide support and enable representation, and some are unable to support such representation. Rob stresses the importance of finding people who demonstrate the potential and interest to support voices from under-represented communities, whether that's from staff networks or elsewhere. He encourages leaders to invest in these people if they aren't already there.

Going into the pandemic with the mindset of improving race equality supported the growth of the partnership's REN movement. When public health reports of the data confirming what was already known about the disproportionate impact of Covid-19 on minority communities were released, the ICS felt able to challenge by asking what could be done about it. West Yorkshire ICS commissioned Dame Donna Kinnair to independently review the impact of Covid-19 on BAME communities and staff (Kinnair, 2020). The review sought to address whether existing work was sufficient to address this impact and to identify further recommendations for the partnership board to implement. This required the ICS to be honest with itself whilst also hearing some difficult truths about where it needed to improve. The ICS prioritized risk assessments for minority communities given that the impact of Covid-19 was worse in these communities.

At the time of the review, Dame Kinnair was the CEO of the RCN. She is recognized as a national figure of influence, having been listed in the 2020 Powerlist, which highlights the hundred most influential Britons of African/African Caribbean descent. In the review, Dame Kinnair commented on the region's vibrant culture, the diversity amongst communities and identities, and the need to facilitate a much-needed conversation to build on what the partnership had already started. She highlighted the genuine commitment from the partnership itself and the strong action-oriented approach to tackling race inequalities. But further work was required. The key recommendations from the report were to:

- improve access to safe work for people
- ensure the partnership's leadership is reflective of communities
- use information to develop culturally competent services aimed at meeting the needs of different groups whilst contributing towards reducing inequalities
- reduce inequalities in mental health outcomes by ethnicity.

The review further detailed how these aims could be achieved, which makes it a useful report for those interested in racial and health inequalities. The recommendations became the basis of an action plan for the partnership and were used as a progress measure at each board meeting as it worked towards the strategic priority of improving race equality. To ensure accountability, the board publishes progress reports on its website to both measure its own progress and be transparent in what it does. The partnership also aimed to strengthen the role of voluntary, charity and social enterprises in the partnership to engage with communities who may not be aware of this work. It further committed to continuing to strengthen the role of the Partnership's REN in delivering change both across the ICS and locally in each place. Rob was keen to ensure that the report and its recommendations were not forgotten, so the agenda item is addressed at public board meetings to keep the partnership and the public aware of what progress measures are being delivered on and how this is being done.

Most of the work has been led by the regional REN network and supported by the partnership leadership team and a voluntary, community and social enterprise (VCSE) subgroup. The group consists of REN network chairs from across the partnership, as well as allies of the race equality agenda. The network focused on using its collective lived experience and knowledge to develop key strands of work focusing on issues affecting staff across the area. These included:

- recruitment, selection and succession planning
- talent, culture and organizational development
- reporting on measurement and impact
- influencing decision-making
- health inequalities
- the award-winning Root Out Racism movement
- the award-winning programme, The Fellowship.

The partnership developed a system leadership development programme known as The Fellowship (West Yorkshire Health and Care Partnership, 2020). The Fellowship was designed and developed by minority ethnic colleagues and aims to provide talented colleagues with the leadership skills and opportunities required to progress their career. The Fellowship provided career coaching, associated competencies to complete and stretch opportunities through funded placements in different settings across the partnership.

At the same time, globally, race equality was brought to the forefront following the murder of George Floyd in the US. And whilst we saw many people condemning his murder, four years down the line, there is not the same appetite for addressing racism. People have forgotten about it, and we have gone back to the same situation. Rob is therefore keen to ensure consistent delivery of the work towards improving race equality and ensure that momentum is not lost but continues to be strengthened through keeping it as a standing item on the partnership's board's agenda. There are two reasons for this: one is to be accountable for what the partnership delivers, and the second goes back to an event that occurred during the launch of Dame Kinnair's report in October 2020.

The report launch took place virtually due to Covid-19 restrictions. The findings of the report were shared, and Dame Kinnair, Rob Webster and several high-profile leaders, including Robin Tuddenham, CEO for Calderdale Council, shared their thoughts, findings and commitments following the publication of the review. The partnership was proud that it had conducted the review and was positive about what had been identified and what was to come. The VCSE sector provided some thoughts and challenge too. The atmosphere was positive and congratulatory until Sheila, a woman from Leeds, spoke. Sheila said that she didn't believe that this report would impact her community, and she could not see how it would be different from previous initiatives. Rob coined the 'Sheila test' – a test to measure whether we are making progress according to people representative of the communities we serve like Sheila.

On the back of that, good governance demanded that the chair of the ICS agree it was a priority, which came from addressing race equality as one of the partnership's strategic priorities (West Yorkshire Health and Care Partnership, 2023b). The strategic priorities recognize the importance of tackling racial inequality, giving the subject as much importance as tackling cancer, maternal mortality and mental health (which also have higher rates of prevalence amongst minority communities).

Another of Dame Kinnair's recommendations was to become an anti-racist system. In response to this, the partnership decided to take time to understand what this meant. It worked towards developing awareness on the issue and then implementing steps towards becoming anti-racist. This became the popular Root Out Racism movement, with almost 600 organizations signing up to the anti-racism pledge that the partnership developed (West Yorkshire Health and

Care Partnership, 2021). It was co-created by over a hundred BAME colleagues across the partnership. It aimed to proactively challenge racism across all aspects of society, to improve health inequalities and to help individuals and organizations to become actively anti-racist. It prompted people to challenge themselves and others around them to better inform themselves on anti-racist behaviours, to tackle racism and to take steps towards meaningful change. Phase 1 consisted of a focus group across the area to understand lived experiences of racism. This insight was formulated and used to develop and launch the Root out Racism movement (campaign) across the ICS's area.

Creating an anti-racism movement

The inspiring Root out Racism movement created a sense of belonging, feeling heard and feeling valued for those involved. It was popular across the region, with hundreds of colleagues using the anti-racism resources across the partnership. However, the movement does not fix all issues around race equality. The prevalence of racism still comes to light, as it did in 2021, when Yorkshire Cricket Club, one of the prominent signatories of the anti-racism movement was embroiled in a high-profile case of racial discrimination faced by one of its employees, Azeem Rafiq. The case was disturbing, as was its handling by the organization involved. Rob reached out to the organization to hold it to account for signing the pledge but acting contradictorily. Support and resources were provided to the organization, but the incident demonstrated that whilst the movement is a start in addressing racism, we still have a long way to go in achieving equity. It also demonstrated that people may sign up to pledges and commitments when their actual work to meet these commitments is still far behind where it needs to be.

Signatories were provided with training and resources with the assumption that work to become anti-racist would need to be undertaken and that signing up to the pledge was only the beginning. It was recognized that this work takes time to embed and implement. When situations exposing dire racism – which has significant consequences – happen, we must address them with transparency and learn as the process continues.

The partnership is making visible progress, with The Fellowship programme seeing tremendous success. The programme has had a 300 per cent increase in applications in three years, with a significant number of applications attaining promotions during or after The Fellowship. The Fellowship is now on to its third cohort, and Rob recently met with participants to talk about leadership. Colleagues partaking in the programme are from various organizations across the partnership, including social housing, NHS and the charity sector. This promotes a wider base for placements and networking for fellows, as well as supporting diversity in leadership across the health and care system, not just the NHS.

When designing The Fellowship, Rob recalls that many attendees expressed how they felt that further training wasn't what was required; rather, they needed the experience and exposure to environments where they could demonstrate their skills. The Fellowship provided this experience through a series of workshops and a one-day-a-week placement. This filled the gap in attaining experience but also benefitted the ICS by providing time and resources to work on projects that otherwise struggled with resources or capacity. Rob thinks that seeing the visible cohort of leadership fellows will be really inspiring for future generations, because of the key aspect of representation: 'You be what you see.'

Whilst the proactive approach taken by the partnership has made some progress in representation across senior leadership, I challenged Rob about the top layer of leadership within the ICS. The ICS board is made up of executives and non-executives, and all executives are of white background. I recognize that just having a BAME person in a position of power does not necessarily signify integrity, leadership or lived experience that reflects those who are under-represented. And many white people are allies who champion the cause of race equality far more than some BAME people. However, it is still an issue, and my goal is to provide that opportunity for the under-represented BAME people with lived experience to be able to aspire to and achieve such roles.

To address this, Rob described his model of distributed leadership. There are people in the ICS who take accountability. For example, Rob is accountable for reducing waiting lists. But responsibility for this lies with West Yorkshire Association of Acute Trusts, where one of the CEOs is Foluke Ajayi, who is a black female. When looking at place-level leadership, the person leading on children's services across Bradford is of BAME background. Most of the membership of the ICB itself as a board is pre-populated, as the membership reflects the services provided, such as the acute trusts' association, the council and housing. Where this was not required, such as in the non-executive director space, Rob liaised closely with recruitment agencies to suggest that their recruitment processes may need to be reviewed to encourage people of under-represented backgrounds to apply.

We spoke about the challenges of applying for senior roles in organizations like the NHS. Rob reflected that sometimes the dos and don'ts of applying for roles are not always clear. There is a presumption that most people understand how things should be done, but it is not always well understood. For example, are you allowed to ring the chair and CEO in advance for a conversation? What should and shouldn't you say in the covering statement? What should your CV look like? Can you talk to people in the ICS in advance to understand the place and whether you can see yourself working there? Many people who apply for roles wouldn't hesitate to do the above, but if someone isn't aware of the expectations, how can they perform and present themselves as an optimum candidate?

Rob is keen to have lived experience from under-represented backgrounds on interview panels. He tries to ensure that the shortlisting and longlist panels are as diverse as possible. There are blind applications, where names and identifiable information are anonymized. An EDI expert then challenges potential applicants on how they will approach the EDI agenda and how they will deliver the ambition of having diverse, representative leadership. The process needed redefining a few times. The persistence paid off, eventually leading to the recruitment of the youngest independent chair in the country, who was female. Amongst the non-executive members is a 20-year-old medical student from a diverse background.

Whether executives were champions or allies was considered, which brought to light the fact that allyship does not always look a certain way. For example, Jonathon Webb, Director of Finance, is a white man but has a team that is exemplary in its finance and functions, cultural competence and work to be an ally in race equality. Work still needs to be done, and Rob wants there to be more visible diversity, not just at executive level but right through the ICS and the various organizations that make up the ICS. This is one of the reasons why the partnership has adopted an inclusive recruitment process.

Leadership and diversity

For Rob, diversity matters. I asked him why and he said that he sees diversity as a strength because it is. The Harvard Business Review highlights the benefits of diversity in leadership teams, including being more objective about facts, considering wider perspectives when decision-making and being more likely to develop new ideas, thereby expanding innovation (Rock and Grant, 2016). When the board has not been representative enough of under-represented groups, the ICS has implemented shadow boards. REN members were part of the shadow board, meaning that there was a seat for an REN representative to attend the SLEG. The papers were sent to members of the REN, who were able to comment and provide their input, which was formulated and presented by the REN representative. The power to influence decisions was provided by ensuring the seat at the SLEG. Having that kind of insight is a powerful mirror that benefits the board by providing input from diverse perspectives from under-represented groups on issues facing the ICS. For REN representatives, it provided the opportunity for exposure to influencing and decision-making at senior leadership level, as well as providing experience to support development that may not otherwise have been accessible. One insight from a REN member who regularly commented on the papers was that they appreciated being able to influence system-level decision-making, where the impact of their input made a difference to not just a few hundred people but thousands across the region.

Reflecting on this with Rob reminds me that the power that senior leaders have can be taken for granted. Senior roles hold power, and you can share this power with others by giving them permission whilst being humble enough to learn from them and bringing them on the journey with you. Listening to what people relay in REN meetings and then acting on it requires a level of humility. The best leaders that Rob has learned from are those who are humble enough to learn from others, be open to criticism and be open to reflecting on and changing how they respond to a situation.

Some leaders struggle with this. Leadership in the NHS was reviewed in the 2000s when the predominant leadership styles were directive or pace-setting (Storey and Holti, 2013). This was driven by a government that sent central targets for services to deliver. That worked for a period, but it set a culture of being directive most of the time. And sometimes directive leadership is not the best style to deploy. The best leader is the one who can demonstrate a range of leadership styles and adapt these to a situation as and when required. A consistently directive style can lead to one-dimensional thinking, which does not allow for fallacy and humility. It then becomes difficult for leaders to ask for support or show compassion, as they can't demonstrate flexibility in their style of leadership.

As the NHS moves towards compassionate leadership styles, there is now much more understanding and acceptance of saying, 'I don't know,' or, 'I got that wrong.' This brings connection, breaks down barriers and promotes a more compassionate approach to dealing with issues (West and Bailey, 2022). Rob learns the most from leaders who can see the bigger picture but also appreciate and review the finer detail. When there are specific complaints or incidents that don't look right, the leader will start to understand the issues by addressing the concerns and having conversations about them. Rob explains that he tends to introduce the issue by saying what is happening and why. For example, if a colleague is behaving in a certain way, he takes the time to understand why they may be doing this. He checks whether they are okay, as there could be something they need support with, whether personally or professionally. If there are no issues, and their behaviour is how they are as a person, this is perhaps when a conversation around performance and expectations should take place. As for supporting staff, Rob says it's about asking questions like are the basic foundations being provided? Do they have the right kit and the right information? Are they in the right place? Do they feel supported? Are they being paid on time? It's important to ensure that people across all levels of the ICS are managed well, almost allowing others to manage whilst you support them from behind.

When information is cascaded down from leadership structures to individual teams, it can become distorted or filtered as it passes down, causing challenges in understanding what the original message was. There is a whole heap of presumption, perception and racism that can get in the way. The first solution for resolving this is being consistent – continue to go back and address the issue. Always use reinforcement when something good happens. This is why the previous trust Rob led had structured listening events with staff. The board would not speak at these events and instead would focus on listening to others. The rich information collated from hearing people's experiences made the board members reflect on and think about what they could do better. Consistency in listening to people and providing safe spaces for them to share what they want supports trust-building and transparency. The second consideration is mentoring programmes. Reciprocal mentoring where strong relationships are built between mentees helps build connections between people. For Rob, one of the successes of reciprocal mentoring lies in it providing a safe space for a conversation to facilitate learning – for both taking part.

The ICS recognizes that progress is not linear. It is dependent on various factors and may change as at the time of writing, the UK prepares itself for a general election; a new government may bring new priorities. Whilst there has been demonstrable improvement in tackling institutional racism in the NHS in some areas, there is still a long way to go. For Rob, some of the great work is in allyship training and support, with 200 people signing up to support cultural competency and mental health development and introducing independent panels at disciplinary panels. Rob wants to be able to see a visible difference and progress on the action plan developed following Dame Kinnair's review in five years' time. He wants the partnership to be known for recognizing talent, providing opportunities and being a place where everyone is welcome. He wants EDI to be everyone's issue, not just the concern of the person who is employed in the role of EDI lead.

Tackling inequalities can feel like a struggle at times and can take an emotional and mental toll. But to hear a leader speak with humility and have a proactive approach and the courage to try and change things offers hope when the journey ahead looks bleak. It is also important to reflect on the changes that have occurred already. In the five years since committing to improve racial inequalities, the REN has achieved considerable successes. The network first brought together all the chairs of the RENs across West Yorkshire. This provided a networking platform, as well as peer support, ideas and accountability amongst chairs for what they should be doing and how they could do it. It then developed a framework to work from. Skills like influencing and networking with network chairs and senior leadership have led to the implementation of a vast array of programmes tackling racial inequality, with specific programmes for staff development (i.e., The Fellowship) and patient experiences (providing input at service design meetings).

There is no doubt that racism and inequalities exist. But if we focus on their existence, we become powerless to tackling them. If we focus on changing them, working together and breaking down barriers, then they will improve as we persist. And we see this already with successful initiatives in West Yorkshire ICB: in the last few years particularly, there has been a rise in the number of people who are speaking up about the importance of diversity and are committed to tackling inequalities. The ICS uses the Core20PLUS5 (West Yorkshire Health and Care Partnership, n.d.) model – a national approach to tackling inequalities that is being embedded in service design for people to benefit from (NHS England, 2022). The ICS REN has been instrumental in holding the leadership to account, challenging where necessary and having the opportunity to not only speak but also be heard. There have been innovative approaches like attending the SLEG, reciprocal mentoring, developing The Fellowship programme and engagement from and with senior leaders and executives across the ICS. The network has had significant influence on providing feedback upwards but also 'down' the chain as well, through bringing together network chairs to develop and lead on initiatives more locally. And whilst there is still a long way to go, there has been some tangible success to date. The challenges ahead are unknown, but there has been some change from where the ICS was when it began.

Whether or not that change will filter down is tricky to determine at present. Change of this nature takes time. In some areas, pockets of work have been achieved. REN members have had the opportunity to influence regional decision-making and policies by inputting on the papers. My personal experience of going from influencing one to ten people as a physiotherapist, to influencing hundreds to thousands of people as a project manager, to potentially influencing millions of people through contributing to papers and how services are designed has been empowering. However, I recognize that without my own willingness to put myself forward, little would have changed. There are times when this work is challenging. But I remember 'why' I do it and keep the public interest at the forefront of what we do. More specifically, I want to see an improvement in representation of people who look like me. I want people who are affected by their circumstances to the extent that it impacts their health to be able to make some of the changes necessary to see improvements in their quality of life. I want them to be empowered to be able to make these changes but also to see a society that actively supports them in doing so.

As someone who has always had strong ambitions, at times it felt unlikely that I would be able to work or influence at senior level. As I reflected on the interviews with Rob and others I spent time with as I wrote this book, I realized what I have achieved to date through being relentless in pursuing my ambitions and hard work. Sometimes it felt unsustainable. But I don't regret it, as it paid off. And I think that my question for anyone reading this and wondering whether it is possible for them would be: If you do not try, then how will you ever know?

It does get tiring, and it can be draining at times. And this is where networking comes in. I come from a background where I was not taught how to network in a professional space. Having learned its importance and seen the success of its application, I have gained confidence in networking. It takes time to learn and practise, and sometimes you may well fail at it. My advice is: be comfortable with getting things wrong. And this is one of the refreshing things about Rob's leadership: he admits that sometimes mistakes are made but says that the important question is: what will we do about it?

There are pockets of work nationally where efforts to improve race equality are excellent, and these are examples to learn from. For example, Leicestershire Partnership NHS Trust spent 18 months developing initiatives to improve racial inequalities at the trust (Bhalla, 2020), including:

- a public anti-racism campaign led by the CEO
- reverse mentoring programmes

- action learning sets for BAME staff to share lived experiences for group reflection
- mandating diverse representation on interview panels
- driving education and training for all staff on their career path
- regular listening events with BAME colleagues to co-design an action plan.

The workforce race inequalities report of 2020 also highlighted three NHS trusts that implemented similar interventions to address race inequalities (Ross *et al.*, 2020). This included establishing staff networks, ensuring psychologically safe routes for raising issues and enabling staff development and career progression. How this looks in each trust will vary, which is why it is essential to undertake listening exercises and build a team that is committed to tackling racial inequalities within the organization.

West Yorkshire has won several awards for the work done around improving race equality and inclusion; however, Rob believes that just because West Yorkshire has won awards in this space doesn't mean they are doing a better job than others. There is always learning to do, and the region still isn't where it wants to be. There are several initiatives that can be considered to improve race equality in NHS trusts, but one size does not fit all. Each trust will have its own unique individual challenges, so taking the time to speak with staff and understand what would work and where you can start from is a good place to begin. The questions below may also help as a starting point.

Reflective questions

* Have you considered what health inequalities may exist in your field? What can you do to change this?
* As a leader, how do you ensure that there is equity within the workplace?
* Are you part of an REN, as either an ally or a network member? Have you ever met with your race equality lead

to ask what issues concern them and how you may be able to help?

* If you are in a board-level position, do you sponsor any RENs? If not, would you consider sponsoring one?

* Consider the initiatives listed in the above case study. Are any present in your organization? If not, could you look into starting one of the initiatives?

— CHAPTER 12 —

Final Thoughts

In this book, I have spoken about the experiences of ethnic minorities, as well as sharing perspectives from allies in race equality. The experiences I've shared were collated through interviews conducted with these individuals, and it was eye-opening to hear the lived experiences of individuals in the NHS. I wanted to understand the experiences of allies too, since race equality is often presented as an issue that BAME people need to deal with, when in fact it is a societal issue that transcends class and colour despite it disproportionately impacting BAME people. Some of the interviews were tough to conduct, especially when I was listening to the difficult experiences people have lived through.

One thing that continues to amaze me even as I write this closing chapter is the inherent sense of wanting to contribute to helping people that we see in the NHS. Without doubt, the healthcare system continues to function because of the goodwill of people who stay over, work late and cover various shifts in order to continue to provide services for those in need. However, in the long term, this is unsustainable, and since the Covid-19 pandemic, many people are exhausted, burnt out and deciding that they can no longer sustain it. The chronic underfunding and understaffing has led to burnout, so people are leaving in droves or needing to take long periods of time off to recover mentally, emotionally and physically from the demanding work they do.

Better support systems are needed, and in some ways the NHS has been striving to achieve this in the form of providing wellbeing training, counselling support and several online resources designed to support people with working in healthcare. Apps that support mental health, such as Headspace, are provided for free. Schwartz Rounds are held in some trusts, providing a space for listening and reflection on difficult experiences and the emotional and social aspects of healthcare. This provides a structured forum for colleagues of all backgrounds to contribute to topics and hear different perspectives.

In this final chapter, I hope to provide advice that supports anyone looking to progress their career and practical tips to support your career journey. In my own career, I recall feeling stuck and desiring a change but not being sure whom to approach or what to do. I felt disheartened when other colleagues were progressing and spoke of being offered roles by managers when that never really happened to me. I believe that a variety of factors led to this, one of which was that I didn't have much of a network to discuss issues with, but I would also undersell my achievements or ambitions. I studied what was happening around me when others were progressing and I wasn't (and wanted to), and I decided to do what I could do to change my situation. I used the following tips during my own journey and have no doubt that they contributed to my success.

Networking

Learn how to network with people. Networking can feel uncomfortable if you have not done it before, but it has the potential to bring many benefits and opportunities. Having a wider network with whom I could communicate provided me with a group of people who could share advice, guidance, opportunities for development and sometimes a listening ear. I heard about and applied for roles that I otherwise would not have been aware of, which supported my career development. I gained a reputation for the good work I had done and had people to seek advice from and talk to in times of difficulty. Networking presented opportunities that I may not otherwise have been able to access.

When I first started networking, it was a daunting experience. I was not used to talking about myself, my work-related interests or what my future plans were. If I wanted to succeed at networking, being able to communicate this information effectively would be useful. For someone who perhaps isn't so confident when engaging with others or an introvert, it can be nerve-wracking to introduce yourself to people you don't know and ask for their help or support.

Thankfully, there are lots of resources online that can give you a better understanding of this subject. After a spot of reading on networking, I developed a pitch and would introduce myself with the following:

> Hi, my name is *name*, *role*. My role involves *brief description of what I do*. I am interested in *area of interest* and would be grateful if we could discuss it further.

This isn't what I said word for word, and I would advise you to adapt it to your character and who you are as a person (sincerity means everything when you are connecting with other people), but it should give a good starting point for those looking to get into networking, as it reads well in emails but is also a short, concise and clear introduction to use when meeting people. When networking, you want to introduce yourself and your role, give a very brief description of what this involves and then say how you think the other person can help you (or you could help them).

Once you have your pitch, be selective in what you want from people and don't be shy to ask! You don't know who is willing or able to offer what, and the only way you find out is by asking people. As for whom to network with, I would say anyone and everyone. It is amazing what you can learn from other people (even people you think you may not learn from) and you never know which connection or relationship will come to fruition. Keeping an open mind is always helpful too. I developed many of my connections through networking, some of whom are now close friends and some of whom have been a lifeline in supporting this book.

Find a mentor

Looking for a mentor was life-changing for me. I learned so much by contacting mentors, and I have no doubt that reaching out to my first mentor was one of the best decisions I've ever made. I learned a lot from someone who had more experience than I did, and there were times when she advised me on decisions that without her support could have been disastrous. Having that guidance from someone more experienced and learning from their journey paid dividends for my learning and development. I believe that the right mentor is someone who becomes a friend and is a good sounding board. My mentors (I still have more than one) would provide me with support, listen to me when I needed to rant, provide advice when I needed guidance and open up opportunities for me that I otherwise wouldn't have come across.

When looking for a mentor, make sure you find someone you get on well with and feel you can learn from. Perhaps a 'role model' – if you like the phrase. In mentoring, personal experiences may be shared when being vulnerable. It can become awkward when listening to personal experiences, and you want to ensure you are able to manage this. There are plenty of resources online to support the mentoring process (e.g., information on how to find a good mentor and how to get the best out of mentoring) and I used resources from Blackpool Teaching Hospitals NHS Foundation Trust and NHS Scotland to inform what mentoring should look like for me. Whilst I initially drafted mentoring contracts (mainly for formality), when you get the right mentor, that contract stuff doesn't really matter because you naturally develop a strong working relationship with that person. But if it doesn't go as well as expected, that's when you can (thankfully) refer to that contract and make an exit if required.

Understand the 'art of influencing'

Influencing is the art of being able to encourage others to help you in achieving what you want. If I was being pessimistic, I would say it's almost like manipulating people; however, this isn't always done for negative purposes. It can mean influencing people to achieve support for wider goals or causes, for example, influencing your managers or supervisees to achieve what is required for the benefit of patients or staff. At a wider political level, influencing is what instigates social change.

For me, learning to influence others was about being able to persuade people why they should listen to what I had to say and why they should do what was being proposed. For some people, this comes naturally. For others, it requires a bit of work, but researching how to influence can be helpful. One of the best books I read on this was *How to Win Friends and Influence People* by Dale Carnegie (2006). This is a practical and interesting read on relationship dynamics, and tips from this book really did make a difference in my relationship building and being able to 'influence' others.

Some people may think they don't have any influence, but this is not true. Everyone has a 'circle of influence' whether it is amongst family or friends or in the workplace. If you take the time to reflect on your life circumstances, you will see whom you are influencing and who is influencing you. Understanding both factors is hugely beneficial in being able to work out what it is you want and, more importantly, how you can go about achieving it by influencing others.

It is important to remember that influencing can be very much trial and error. You won't always be able to influence everyone (probably because someone else is doing it just a bit better than you; this is fine – you won't be the best at everything, every time, in every situation).

Excel in what you do

Whatever your specialism, expertise or line of work, make it your mission to be the very best at what you do. Striving to be knowledgeable in your field is always well received, because it shows your dedication, passion and commitment to what you turn up to do every day. The best way to gain this knowledge is through reading and being well informed in your field. For example, when I worked in physiotherapy, I would spend extra time reading up on evidence in that area, networking with experienced colleagues to ask questions to further my understanding and reflecting with curiosity on how we could improve services to benefit patients. This meant that I developed a reputation for having a keen eye for service improvement, which subsequently helped me to develop other connections, explore other opportunities and meet some amazing people in my career – things that wouldn't have happened if I hadn't demonstrated this drive and vision to excel in what I do.

In my opinion, the number-one way to excel is to be well informed on matters that interest you. If you work in healthcare, for example, read up on issues that impact your ward (i.e., funding, staffing, service improvement initiatives from other trusts). Through reading, you can develop the confidence to contribute to discussions because you have the knowledge required to partake effectively in such conversations.

You are more likely to be heard when presenting a well-informed opinion (because, let's face it, no one likes someone who waffles on about stuff they don't know). You need to have the confidence to articulate your view, so talking with others about what you have read or understand helps. Talking to others about a topic in a way that they can comprehend will help you to solidify your understanding of and give you confidence in your topic. There isn't much point in being well versed in a topic if you're not able to relate that understanding to others. You must be able to communicate in a way that people understand so they do not have to work hard to interpret your message.

Push yourself out of your comfort zone

Life begins at the edge of one's comfort zone, so do things you would not normally do to grow your skills and development. It is from here that one progresses one's skills, experiences and interests as a person. Sometimes we are conditioned to stick with the status quo and taught not to rock the boat. Obviously, it depends on the context you find yourself in, but rocking the boat is sometimes necessary if you can see benefits for patients, the team or your development. If you attempt to leave your comfort zone and fail, don't be disheartened! See it as a learning curve and remember that failure is how you can improve things next time.

The greatest inventors, entrepreneurs and visionaries of our time (such as Thomas Edison and Nelson Mandela) all endured difficulties, hardship or failure before achieving their greatest successes. Edison and Mandela's successes became successes of society that directly and indirectly impact each of us to this day: Edison developed the light bulb and Mandela ended apartheid. Push out of your comfort zone, learn from the opportunities that come with this and keep trying again and again until you achieve the desired outcome. This can be difficult at times, but I like to remember the words of one of my first mentors, 'You will never discover new oceans until you develop the courage to lose sight of the shore' – you need to push off the shore to discover new possibilities.

I am not a fan of being too comfortable in one's role. If someone has been doing the same job for 20 years and is not able to demonstrate how they have developed both personally and professionally within that time, I would question how much improvement can be made in services or within themselves. Looking to develop and reinvent yourself regularly, whether that's with a change in role or a change in department, is essential to your personal and professional growth. You can only learn new things from doing this, and it will stop you from getting too attached to organizations and from doing the same thing day in, day out.

Volunteer for opportunities

Volunteer for opportunities when others don't – everyone hates that awkwardness in the room when a manager asks for a task to be completed and no one volunteers. And let's face it, no one likes being volun-told either! Be the one who says yes, because often that will be remembered by others. If and when you require support later on, a good manager will remember that you helped them and return the favour.

Sometimes putting ourselves forward for tasks can be daunting because we worry about whether we will be able to complete them. There isn't anything to stop you from volunteering but also making it clear what elements you require support with. Most people will appreciate your honesty and ability to articulate what you require support with to fulfil the task; plus, seeking the appropriate help in the first place will mean that there will be less chance of you having to redo it.

Volunteering for tasks or opportunities demonstrates a forthcoming, proactive nature, which is always valued in one's personal life as well as in the workplace. It gives you an opportunity to practise your skills and problem-solving abilities by either finding the solutions within yourself or seeking help from others. If you don't have the skillset to complete the task required, this is an opportunity to expand your skillset. And if you are reading this and thinking that you aren't a good problem-solver, perhaps this is an opportunity to develop that skill!

Be confident in selling yourself

Every one of us has a unique set of skills and talents. To discover what these are requires effort and work on your part. It is only by identifying your skills, talents and abilities as an individual that you can be confident in who you are and then sell yourself better.

I have met some incredibly intelligent, articulate people who had the potential to be very successful. But some of them lacked the ability to sell themselves in situations, for example at interview stage for a post they wanted. Sometimes, when we achieve incredible things, we think that in order to remain humble, we shouldn't shout about our achievements. We keep quiet, expecting others to celebrate our successes for us.

Don't leave celebrating your successes, skills or abilities to others, especially if they are something you are proud of. Being invited to Rome to present research on pressure ulcers in therapies was an incredibly proud achievement for me. At the time, I was disappointed that more wasn't made of my success: it was a huge accomplishment, not only for me but also for the department, because no one had achieved this before. I decided to shout about it myself, and when this was recognized by directors and the CEO, I felt proud. Sometimes we think that we shouldn't shout about our achievements because it may come across as arrogant. There is a difference between celebrating success and positivity and being arrogant. It is fine to celebrate your successes as long as you don't think they make you better than others. If you use your successes to put others down or think you are better than them, then that is arrogance. And that's what should be avoided.

So often, we don't sell ourselves enough, but some people know how to talk about and sell themselves well, even if they aren't that good at the task at hand. I'm sure we all know people like that, because they are often the ones who annoy us when we are left picking up their work. In the past, I would be annoyed about these people because they spoke well but did very little. However, I decided to observe how they sold themselves, and I learned that they had an air of confidence and the ability to communicate with others in a way that makes people want to listen to them. Carnegie's book, which I mentioned earlier, covers communication, but many other resources on the art of communication are available too.

Help others
One of the biggest things I think you can do to help yourself is to help others. It truly helps one to grow and stay humble.

Pick your battles
In the world of work, politics will always arise. I used to think that every wrong needs to be corrected, but I was wisely advised early on that learning to pick one's battles is far more effective. The reality is that you won't always change everything or win every time. And that's okay. But just as the art of communication is essential to success, so is the art of knowing when to stay silent.

Listen first, speak last
The best leaders are the ones who listen to what others have to say before offering their own opinions and then asking others for theirs. If you are first to speak and you are in charge, others will often agree just because they don't want to disagree. Or they might agree because they think a solution has already been found rather than thinking outside of the box. If you listen first, it empowers other people, and it may well provide you with an opportunity to learn something different or new before offering your opinion. Others will respect that, it will inform your opinions on a topic and it might give you a better solution before you speak.

Know yourself
It is with these two final words that I end this chapter. Knowing oneself both personally and professionally is very important. It is who we are, what we do and shapes our place in the world. How do you expect to have an impact if you don't know who you are and what you want? Take the time to explore who you are for yourself, and revisit it regularly to ensure that you have a firm grounding in your own sense of self. Tools that can help you get started with this include books on self-development, understanding character types and understanding temperaments.

One of the most important things that I learned about myself is that I am not as patient as I thought I was. As I explored why, I was able to work towards improving that aspect of myself and managing it better when my patience was tested. It also means that when life gets tough, I feel more able to recognize that within myself, so I take the time to relax, enjoy other activities, recharge my batteries and return to what I need to do with a better sense of self and purpose.

At the beginning of this book, I spoke about the power of leadership. We are all leaders in one way or another. But it is only through knowing yourself and understanding your place in the world that you will truly be able to make a difference. And that always comes from within you, no matter what circumstances you are facing or your background. People of ethnic minority background have unique challenges in the NHS, but we must work to identify unique opportunities in order to improve the status quo and strive towards race equality, representative leadership and eliminating discrimination, particularly when it is embedded in institutions and systems.

Acronyms

AHP: Allied health professional
BAME: Black, Asian and minority ethnic
EDI: Equality, diversity and inclusion
ICB: Integrated Care Board
ICS: Integrated Care System
OT: Occupational therapist
REN: Race Equality Network
SLEG: System Leadership Executive Group

Acknowledgements

The Almighty – Indeed, He has been very kind and very generous to me in my life, and I could never thank Him enough for the blessings He has bestowed upon me and my family. Alhamdulillah.

My editing and publishing team, particularly Sarah Hamlin who presented me with this opportunity. Thank you for your commitment, support and patience throughout the development of this book. A huge thank you to Masooma Malik for her support and awesome editing skills throughout this journey.

My Grandad (nana) – A man full of wisdom and depth, may God have mercy on his soul.

My father – One of the most selfless individuals I know, who has always been a guiding force in my education, progress and success. Thank you for all you have done for us and continue to do.

Sunita Sokhal – Literally would not be able to live it down if I wrote a book and did not include your name! The best OT I have ever worked with, the Bonnie and Clyde of Therapies. So many memories with you, and honoured to say I still learn from you to this day.

Nabila Akhtar – For your unwavering support, faith and encouragement. And endless patience and support with me when sharing my frustrations. Thank you.

Brian Chiyesu – Thank you for your encouragement, your advice and your guidance in helping me to navigate the minefield of leadership and race equality. It's been an honour to work with you and I pray you forever remain on the path of justice.

Tuba Mazhari – For your encouragement, support and 'can-do'

attitude. You were one of the early inspirers who encouraged me to start this book, and what a journey it has been!

Naima Roberts – Without your sound advice and guidance, this book would probably never have come to fruition. I still remember your words of encouragement that one night during Ramadan; you have probably forgotten them but they are etched into the memory of my heart and mind. Forever grateful for your words.

Julie Mansfield – For always being a huge supporter, confidante, friend and manager. Thank you.

Nicola Roberts – Thank you for your ever-encouraging words of advice, your ability to coach me and your uplifting support in my difficult times.

Rachel Stewart – Top manager, great mentor and a trusted friend. Thank you so much for your support both personally and professionally.

Sundus Pasha – Thank you so much for your guidance, encouragement and above all, friendship. Without a doubt, you were one of the drivers of this book!

Khadija Azeem – A shining star with the heart of a lion. You inspire me every day and I am always so proud of you. May God always bless you, protect you and grant you every form of goodness!

Shahab Adris – Thank you for seeing my potential at a time when I didn't think I had any. Your support, encouragement and unwavering persistence in helping us strive to achieve is one of the reasons for my success. Thank you.

The MEND community – For providing people like me with the ambition and hope that we can achieve what we want to, despite the odds, and for providing inspiring role models who continue to do so.

To all who have participated in the making of this book, it was a privilege to listen to your stories and I will forever be grateful for you giving your time and honesty in sharing your experiences with me.

To all my friends and family who have supported me throughout the journey of writing this book, thank you.

To all those who have been part of my life journey, thank you. In whatever capacity it has been, you have no doubt served as part of this journey, and without the opportunity to have such experiences, this book probably would never have materialized. Thank you.

References

Chapter 1

BBC. (2020). Craig Whittaker: MP defends saying some Muslims not taking covid seriously. BBC, 31 July 2020. www.bbc.co.uk/news/uk-politics-53612230.

Brain, J. (2021). The birth of the NHS. Budleigh Salterton: Historic UK. www.historic-uk.com/HistoryUK/HistoryofBritain/Birth-of-the-NHS.

Bulut, M. (2023). Key statistics on the NHS. London: NHS Confederation. www.nhsconfed.org/articles/key-statistics-nhs.

Butler, P. (2022). Black and minority ethnic people in UK twice as likely to be in 'deep poverty'. *The Guardian*, 6 October 2022. www.theguardian.com/society/2022/oct/06/black-and-minority-ethnic-people-in-uk-twice-as-likely-to-be-in-deep-poverty.

Campbell, D. (2016). Nye Bevan's dream: a history of the NHS. *The Guardian*, 18 January 2016. www.theguardian.com/society/2016/jan/18/nye-bevan-history-of-nhs-national-health-service.

Department of Health and Social Care. (2023). The NHS Constitution for England. London: Department of Health and Social Care. www.gov.uk/government/publications/the-nhs-constitution-for-england.

Diversity UK. (2023). Census 2021 data reveals ethnic make up of UK population. Borehamwood: Diversity UK. https://diversityuk.org/census-2021-data-reveals-ethnic-make-up-of-uk-population/#:~:text=According%20to%20the%202021%20Census,increase%20from%2013.8%25%20in%202011.

Ethnic Dimension. (2014). *Identifying and Removing Barriers to Talented BAME Staff Progression in the Civil Service.* Windsor: Ethnic Dimension. https://assets.publishing.service.gov.uk/media/5a74b356e5274a3f93b48174/Ethnic_Dimension_Blockages_to_Talented_BAME_staff_Progression_in_the_Civil_Service_Final_16.12.14__1_.pdf.

Giebel, C., McIntyre, J. C., Daras, K., Gabbay, M., et al. (2019). What are the social predictors of accident and emergency attendance in disadvantaged neighbourhoods? Results from a cross-sectional household health survey in the north west of England. *BMJ Open 9*, 1, e022820. https://doi.org/10.1136/bmjopen-2018-022820.

Kline, R., Martin, B. (2013). *Discrimination By Appointment: How Black and Minority Ethnic Applicants Are Disadvantaged in NHS Staff Recruitment.* London: Public World Ltd.

Muslim Engagement and Development. (2017). Employment discrimination against Muslims. www.mend.org.uk/wp-content/uploads/2017/10/Employment-Discrimination-against-Muslims.pdf.

NHS Digital. (2022). NHS Workforce Statistics. Leeds: NHS Digital. https://digital.nhs.uk/data-and-information/publications/statistical/nhs-workforce-statistics/june-2022.

NHS England. (2023). *NHS Workforce Race Equality Standard (WRES) 2022 Data Analysis Report for NHS Trusts*. Redditch: NHS England. www.england.nhs.uk/long-read/nhs-workforce-race-equality-standard-wres2022-data-analysis-report-for-nhs-trusts.

Platt, L., Warwick, R. (2020). *Are Some Ethnic Groups More Vulnerable to Covid-19 than Others?* London: Institute for Fiscal Studies. https://ifs.org.uk/sites/default/files/output_url_files/Are-some-ethnic-groups-more-vulnerable-to%252520COVID-19-than-others-V2-IFS-Briefing-Note.pdf.

Redfish. (2018). The great NHS sell-off. Death by a thousand cuts. Berlin: Redfish. https://archive.org/details/death-by-a-thousand-cuts-the-great-nhs-sell-off-part-1.

Taylor, D. (2023). After the cowardly attack on migrants in Knowsley, a warning to ministers: your words can start fires. *The Guardian*, 13 February 2023. www.theguardian.com/commentisfree/2023/feb/13/attack-migrants-knowsley-ministers-violence-asylum-seekers.

UK Government. (2018). *Independent Report: Race at Work 2018: McGregor-Smith Review – One Year On*. London: UK Government. www.gov.uk/government/publications/race-at-work-2018-mcgregor-smith-review-one-year-on.

West, M. (2020). What does the 2019 NHS Staff Survey truly tell us about how staff needs are being met? London: The Kings Fund. www.kingsfund.org.uk/insight-and-analysis/blogs/2019-nhs-staff-survey-staff-needs-being-met.

Chapter 2

Acas. (2023). Race discrimination. London: Acas. www.acas.org.uk/race-discrimination/types-of-race-discrimination.

Ali, L. (2021). Caribbean women and the NHS. London: Black History Month. www.blackhistorymonth.org.uk/article/section/nhs-and-healthcare/caribbean-women-nhs.

Ashikali, T., Groeneveld, S., Kuipers, B. (2021). The role of inclusive leadership in supporting an inclusive climate in diverse public sector teams. *Review of Public Personnel Administration 41*, 3, 497–519. https://doi.org/10.1177/0734371X19899722.

BMA. (2021). *A Missed Opportunity: BMA Response to the Race Report*. London: British Medical Association.

Calkin, S. (2013). Race 'a factor' in variability of sickle cell services. London: Health Service Journal. www.hsj.co.uk/integrated-care/exclusive-race-a-factor-in-variability-of-sickle-cell-services-/5062800.article.

Chambers, N., Pryce, A., Li, Y., Poljsak, P. (2011). *Spot the Difference: A Study of Boards of High Performing Organisations in the NHS*. Manchester: Manchester Business School.

Commission on Race and Ethnic Disparities. (2021). *Commission on Race and Ethnic Disparities: The Report*. London: UK Government. https://assets.publishing.service.gov.uk/government/uploads/system/uploads/attachment_data/file/974507/20210331_-_CRED_Report_-_FINAL_-_Web_Accessible.pdf.

Dent, E. (2006). Winterton: BME service discrimination 'unethical and unlawful'. London: Health Service Journal. www.hsj.co.uk/home/winterton-bme-service-discrimination-unethical-and-unlawful/2344.article.

Equality and Human Rights Commission. (2016). *Healing a Divided Britain: The Need for a Comprehensive Race Equality Strategy*. London: Equality and Human Rights Commission. www.equalityhumanrights.com/sites/default/files/healing_a_divided_britain_-_the_need_for_a_comprehensive_race_equality_strategy_final.pdf.

Equality and Human Rights Commission. (2020). Race discrimination. London: Equality and Human Rights Commission. www.equalityhumanrights.com/equality/equality-act-2010/your-rights-under-equality-act-2010/race-discrimination.

Fazil, Q. (2018). *Cancer and Black and Minority Ethnic Communities*. London: Race Equality Foundation. pp.1–19.

Francis, R. (2013). *Report of the Mid Staffordshire NHS Foundation Trust Public Inquiry*. London: The Stationery Office. www.gov.uk/government/organisations/mid-staffordshire-nhs-foundation-trust-public-inquiry.

Furness, H. (2012). £1m for NHS manager Elliott Browne who was targeted for his colour. *Daily Telegraph*, 10 January 2012. www.telegraph.co.uk/news/health/news/9003744/1m-for-NHS-manager-Elliot-Browne-who-was-targeted-for-his-colour.html.

Healthcare Commission. (2009). *Tackling the Challenge: Promoting Race Equality in the NHS in England*. London: Commission for Healthcare Audit and Inspection.

Hofhuis, J., van der Rijt, P. G., Vlug, M. (2016). Diversity climate enhances work outcomes through trust and openness in workgroup communication. *Springerplus* 5, 1, 714. https://doi.org/10.1186/s40064-016-2499-4.

Kline, R. (2014). The 'snowy white peaks' of the NHS: a survey of discrimination in governance and leadership and the potential impact on patient care in London and England. www.mdx.ac.uk/__data/assets/pdf_file/0015/50190/The-snowy-white-peaks-of-the-NHS.pdf.pdf.

Knight, M., Bunch, K., Patel, R., Shakespeare, J., et al. (eds) on behalf of MBRRACE-UK. (2022). *Saving Lives, Improving Mothers' Care: Lessons Learned to Inform Maternity Care from the UK and Ireland Confidential Enquiries into Maternal Deaths and Morbidity 2018–20*. Oxford: National Perinatal Epidemiology Unit, University of Oxford. www.npeu.ox.ac.uk/assets/downloads/mbrrace-uk/reports/maternal-report-2022/MBRRACE-UK_Maternal_MAIN_Report_2022_UPDATE.pdf.

Lowe, K. (2020). Five times immigration changed the UK. BBC, 20 January 2020. www.bbc.co.uk/news/uk-politics-51134644.

Marmot, M. (2010). *Fair Society, Healthy Lives: The Marmot Review: Strategic Review of Health Inequalities in England Post-2010*. London: Department for International Development. https://www.gov.uk/research-for-development-outputs/fair-society-healthy-lives-the-marmot-review-strategic-review-of-health-inequalities-in-england-post-2010#Abstract.

Mind. (2020). *Inequalities for Black Asian and Minority Ethnic Communities in NHS Mental Health Services in England*. London: Mind. pp.1–15.

NHS England. (2022). *NHS Workforce Race Equality Standard (WRES) 2022 Data Analysis Report for NHS Trusts*. Redditch: NHS England. www.england.nhs.uk/publication/nhs-workforce-race-equality-standard-2022.

NHS Quality and Diversity Council. (2017). *Workforce Race Equality Standard Data Reporting – March 2017*. Redditch: NHS England. www.england.nhs.uk/publication/workforce-race-equality-standard-data-reporting-march-2017.

Public Accounts Committee. (2014). *Public Accounts Committee – Fortieth Report: Maternity Services in England*. London: UK Parliament. https://publications.parliament.uk/pa/cm201314/cmselect/cmpubacc/776/77602.htm.

Redhead, G. (2021). 'A British problem affecting British people': sickle cell anaemia, medical activism and race in the National Health Service, 1975–1993. *Oxford Academic*, 32, 2, 189–211. https://doi.org/10.1093/tcbh/hwab007.

Strategic Health Authority. (2004). *Race Equality Guide 2004: A performance framework*. London: North Central London Strategic Health Authority on behalf of English Strategic Health Authorities. www.jstor.org/stable/bf205674-5a4a-3048-b53b-892459487c55?seq=2.

Thomson, C., Forman, D. (2009). *Cancer Incidence and Survival by Major Ethnic Group, England, 2002 – 2006*. London: The National Cancer Intelligence Network and Cancer Research UK.

UK Government. (2010). Equality Act 2010. London: The Stationery Office. www.legislation.gov.uk/ukpga/2010/15/introduction.

Watkinson, R. E., Sutton, M., Turner, A. J. (2021). Ethnic inequalities in health-related quality of life among older adults in England: secondary analysis of a national cross-sectional survey. *The Lancet* 6, 3, E145–E154. https://doi.org/10.1016/S2468-2667(20)30287-5.

West, M., Dawson, J., Kaur, M. (2015). *Making the Difference: Diversity and Inclusion in the NHS*. London: The Kings Fund, pp.1–95. www.kingsfund.org.uk/insight-and-analysis/reports/making-difference-diversity-inclusion-nhs.

Wessely, S. (2018). *Modernising the Mental Health Act: Increasing Choice, Reducing Compulsion: Final Report of the Independent Review of the Mental Health Act 1983*. London: Department of Health and Social Care. https://assets.publishing.service.gov.uk/government/uploads/system/uploads/attachment_data/file/778897/Modernising_the_Mental_Health_Act_-_increasing_choice__reducing_compulsion.pdf.

White, N. (2022). Sickle cell: NHS to investigate racial inequalities for first time. *The Independent*, 22 September 2022. www.independent.co.uk/news/health/nhs-sickle-cell-racism-healthcare-b2172388.html.

Williams, W. (2018). *Independent Report: Windrush Lessons Learned Review by Wendy Williams*. London: Home Office. www.gov.uk/government/publications/windrush-lessons-learned-review.

WRES. (2022). *NHS Workforce Race Equality Standard (WRES) 2022 Data Analysis Report for NHS Trusts*. Redditch: NHS England. www.england.nhs.uk/long-read/nhs-workforce-race-equality-standard-wres2022-data-analysis-report-for-nhs-trusts.

Chapter 3

Campbell, D. (2023). Most foreign doctors in NHS face 'racist microaggressions', survey shows. *The Guardian*, 8 November 2023. www.theguardian.com/society/2023/nov/08/more-than-half-of-foreign-doctors-in-nhs-experience-racist-microaggressions.

Gueits, D. (2022). What are microaggressions? Cleveland: Cleveland Clinic. https://health.clevelandclinic.org/what-are-microaggressions-and-examples.

Hollowood, L. (2022). Micro refers to its subtle delivery – not its impact. *Royal College of Nursing Magazine*, 26 October 2022. www.rcn.org.uk/magazines/Advice/2022/October/Microaggressions-calling-out-racism-in-the-workplace.

James-Edwards, D. (2022). Speaking up: challenging microaggressions in the workplace. London: The King's Fund. www.kingsfund.org.uk/blog/2022/12/speaking-challenging-microaggressions-workplace.

Johnson, N. N., Johnson, T. L. (2019). Microaggressions: An Introduction. In U. Thomas (ed.) *Navigating Micro-Aggressions Toward Women in Higher Education* (pp.1–22). Hershey: IGI Global.

Law, M., Cooper, B. A., Strong, S., Stewart, D., Rigby, P., Letts, L. (1996). The person-environment-occupation model: a transactive approach to occupational performance. *Canadian Journal of Occupational Therapy 63*, 9–23.

NHS Employers. (2022). Pay scales for 2022/23. London: NHS Employers. www.nhsemployers.org/articles/pay-scales-202223.

NHS England. (n.d.). Allied Health Professionals. Redditch: NHS England. www.england.nhs.uk/ahp/role.

NHS Leadership Academy. (2024). Noticing and challenging microaggressions. Leeds: NHS Leadership Academy. www.leadershipacademy.nhs.uk/core-managers-noticing-and-challenging-microaggressions.

Pierce, C. M. (1974). Psychiatric Problems of the Black Minority. In S. Arieti (ed.) *American Handbook of Psychiatry* (pp.512–523). New York, NY: Basic Books.

Rastrick, S. (2020). Allied health professional workforce diversity. Redditch: NHS England. www.england.nhs.uk/blog/allied-health-professional-workforce-diversity.

Williams, M. (2020). Microaggressions: clarification, evidence, and impact. *Perspectives on Psychological Science 15*, 1, 3–26. https://journals.sagepub.com/doi/pdf/10.1177/1745691619827499.

Chapter 4

Argyrides, A., Castro-Ayala, A., Borneo, A., Hadden, C., et al. (2023). *Valuing Nursing in the UK*. London: Royal College of Nursing. www.rcn.org.uk/Professional-Development/publications/valuing-nursing-in-the-uk-uk-pub-010-695.

Calkin, S. (2013). Concern over race bias on nurse leadership course. *Nursing Times*, 29 October 2013. www.nursingtimes.net/archive/exclusive-concern-over-race-bias-on-nurse-leadership-course-29-10-2013.

Kahin, M., Khan, N. (2023). Healthcare inequalities and social justice blog series: transcultural leadership, anti-racism, and psychological safety. *British Medical Journal Blogs*, October 18, 2023. https://blogs.bmj.com/bmjleader/2023/10/18/transcultural-leadership-anti-racism-and-psychological-safety-by-by-mushtag-kahin-and-dr-nagina-khan.

Kline, R. (2014). The 'snowy white peaks' of the NHS: a survey of discrimination in governance and leadership and the potential impact on patient care in London and England. www.mdx.ac.uk/__data/assets/pdf_file/0015/50190/The-snowy-white-peaks-of-the-NHS.pdf.

Launder, M. (2020). Voices of change: speaking up about racial inequality. London: Nursing in Practice. www.nursinginpractice.com/analysis/voices-of-change-speaking-up-about-racial-inequality.

Palmer, B., Rolewicz, L. (2022). Peak leaving? A spotlight on nurse leaver rates in the UK. London: Nuffield Trust. www.nuffieldtrust.org.uk/resource/peak-leaving-a-spotlight-on-nurse-leaver-rates-in-the-uk.

Sprinks, J. (2014). Vision of BME nurse leaders 'from wards to boards' still long way off. *Nursing Standard 28*, 22, 12–22. https://journals.rcni.com//doi/abs/10.7748/ns2014.01.28.22.12.s14.

Chapter 5

Dago A., Ray, J. (2014). Belief in work ethic strong across Africa. Washington, DC: Gallup. https://news.gallup.com/poll/174263/belief-work-ethic-strong-across-africa.aspx.

Department of Health and Social Care. (2023). The NHS Constitution for England. London: Department of Health and Social Care. www.gov.uk/government/publications/the-nhs-constitution-for-england.

Pemberton, A., Kisamore, J. (2023). Assessing burnout in diversity and inclusion professionals. *Equality, Diversity and Inclusion 42*, 1, 38–52. https://doi.org/10.1108/EDI-12-2020-0360.

Survey Coordination Centre. (2023). *NHS Staff Survey 2022: National Results Briefing*. Oxford: Survey Coordination Centre, Picker Institute Europe.

Taylor, M., Mortimer, D., Walter, S. (2023). NHS Confederation response to Steven Barclay, Secretary of State for Health. www.nhsconfed.org/system/files/2023-10/20.10.23%20-%20NHS%20Confederation%20letter%20to%20The%20Rt%20Hon%20Steve%20Barclay%20MP.pdf.

Chapter 6

Ajilore, O., Thames, A. D. (2020). The fire this time: the stress of racism, inflammation and COVID-19. *Brain, Behaviour and Immunity 88*, 66–67. www.sciencedirect.com/science/article/pii/S0889159120310424?via%3Dihub.

Askin, F. (2009). Chilling Effect. Murfreesboro: Free Speech Center. https://firstamendment.mtsu.edu/article/chilling-effect/#:~:text=Chilling%20effect%20is%20the%20conc.

Baines, E. (2022). Decline in NHS speaking up culture 'very concerning'. *Nursing Times*, 31 March 2022. www.nursingtimes.net/news/workforce/decline-in-nhs-speaking-up-culture-very-concerning-31-03-2022.

Cambridge Dictionary. (2023). Equality Definition. Cambridge: Cambridge University Press & Assessment. https://dictionary.cambridge.org/dictionary/english/equality.

Fenwick, J. (2021). Woke: compliment or criticism, it is now fuelling the culture wars. BBC, 21 August 2021. www.bbc.co.uk/news/uk-politics-58281576.

Francis, R. (2013). *Report of the Mid Staffordshire NHS Foundation Trust Public Inquiry*. London: The Stationery Office. www.gov.uk/government/organisations/mid-staffordshire-nhs-foundation-trust-public-inquiry.

Geronimus, A. T., Hicken, M., Keene, D., Bound, J. (2006). 'Weathering' and age patterns of allostatic load scores among blacks and whites in the United States. *American Journal of Public Health 96*, 5, 826–833. www.ncbi.nlm.nih.gov/pmc/articles/PMC1470581.

Goffee, R., Jones, G. (2006). *Why Should Anyone Be Led by You? What It Takes To Be An Authentic Leader*. Boston: Harvard Business Review Press. p.1.

Gupta, A. H. (2023). How 'weathering' contributes to racial health disparities. *New York Times*, 12 April 2023. www.nytimes.com/2023/04/12/well/live/weathering-health-racism-discrimination.html.

Jarral, F. (2023). Weathering by Arline Geronimus review – how discrimination makes you sick. *The Guardian*, 17 March 2023. www.theguardian.com/books/2023/mar/17/weathering-by-arline-geronimus-review-how-discrimination-makes-you-sick.

Mallorie, S. (2024). Illustrating the relationship between poverty and NHS services. London: The King's Fund. www.kingsfund.org.uk/insight-and-analysis/long-reads/relationship-poverty-nhs-services.

Mind. (2021). Racism and mental health. London: Mind. www.mind.org.uk/information-support/tips-for-everyday-living/racism-and-mental-health/#HowRacismCanAffectYourMentalHealth.

National Association of Colleges and Employers. (2023). Equity Definition. Bethlehem, PA: National Association of Colleges and Employers. www.naceweb.org/about-us/equity-definition#:~:text=The%20term%20%E2%80%9Cequity%E2%80%9D%20refers%20to,and%20make%20adjustments%20to%20imbalances.

NHS England. (2021). *Position Specification: National Health Service: Chief Executive*. Redditch: NHS England. www.england.nhs.uk/wp-content/uploads/2021/05/SPEC-National-Health-Service-Chief-Executive.pdf.

NHS England. (2023). *NHS Workforce Race Equality Standard (WRES): 2022 Data Analysis Report for NHS Trusts*. Redditch: NHS England. www.england.nhs.uk/wp-content/uploads/2023/02/workforce-race-equality-standard.pdf.

NHS Leadership Academy. (2018). *Clinician to Chief Executive: Supporting Leaders of the Future*. London: NHS Providers. https://nhsproviders.org/media/518499/clinician-to-chief-executive-supporting-the-leaders-of-tromorrow_web.pdf.

NHS Leadership Academy. (2023). Programmes. Leeds: NHS Leadership Academy. www.leadershipacademy.nhs.uk/programmes.

NHS Workforce Statistics. (2022). By ethnicity and grade (managers and senior managers). Leeds: NHS Digital. www.ethnicity-facts-figures.service.gov.uk/workforce-and-business/workforce-diversity/nhs-workforce/latest/#by-ethnicity-and-grade-managers-and-senior-managers.

O'Dwyer-Cunliffe, F., Russell, J. (2020). *BAME Representation and Experience in the NHS*. London: NHS Providers.

Patient Safety Learning Hub. (2020). We all want a culture of speaking up, don't we? So, why isn't it happening? London: Patient Safety Learning Hub. www.pslhub.org/learn/culture/bullying-and-fear/we-all-want-a-culture-of-speaking-up-don't-we-so-why-isn't-it-happening-r2318.

Pitcher, G. (2015). So what does it take to be a chief executive in the NHS? London: Health Service Journal. www.hsj.co.uk/workforce/so-what-does-it-take-to-be-a-chief-executive-in-the-nhs/5091689.article.

Public Health England. (2020). *Beyond the Data: Understanding the Impact of COVID-19 on BAME Communities*. London: PHE Publications. https://assets.publishing.service.gov.uk/media/5ee761fce90e070435f5a9dd/COVID_stakeholder_engagement_synthesis_beyond_the_data.pdf.

Schlossberg, J. (2022). How does racism make you sick? Los Angeles: UCLA Health. www.uclahealth.org/news/how-does-racism-make-you-sick.

Silvera, G. A., Clark, J. R. (2021). Women at the helm: chief executive officer gender and patient experience in the hospital industry. *Healthcare Management Review* 46, 3, 206–216. https://journals.lww.com/hcmrjournal/abstract/2021/07000/women_at_the_helm__chief_executive_officer_gender.5.aspx.

Smith, H., Garcia, C. A. (2020). BAME people hold just 4.6% of the UK's most powerful roles, data shows. London: Sky News. https://news.sky.com/story/bame-people-hold-just-4-6-of-the-uks-most-powerful-roles-data-shows-12033268.

Subramaniam, A. (2021). Why lived experience matters. New York: Psychology Today. www.psychologytoday.com/us/blog/parenting-neuroscience-perspective/202109/why-lived-experience-matters.

Syal, R. (2023). Braverman to have Home Office diversity training vetted after 'woke' claims. *The Guardian*, 14 September 2023. www.theguardian.com/politics/2023/sep/14/suella-braverman-to-have-diversity-courses-at-home-office-vetted-after-woke-claims.

Thomas, R. (2020). Executives all white in city where 40pc of population is BAME. London: Health Service Journal. www.hsj.co.uk/university-hospitals-birmingham-nhs-foundation-trust/executives-all-white-in-city-where-40pc-of-population-is-bame/7028334.article.

Timmins, N. (2016). *The Chief Executive's Tale: View from the Front Line of the NHS*. London: The King's Fund.

Wagner, A. J., Tennen, H., Feinn, R., Finan, P. H. (2013). Racial discrimination and metabolic control in women with type 2 diabetes. *Ethnicity and Disease 23*, 4, 421–427. www.jstor.org/stable/48667893.

Wilson, C. (2020). N-word: the troubled history of the racial slur. BBC, 5 October 2020. www.bbc.co.uk/news/stories-53749800.

Chapter 7

Health Education England. (n.d.). *AHP Support Workforce – Grow Your Own Workforce Strategy*. Leeds: Health Education England.

Jasper, R., Wilberforce, M., Abendstern, M., Tucker, S., Challis, D. (2019). Support workers in community mental health teams for older people: exploring sources of satisfaction and stress. *Journal of Long-Term Care*, 111–118.

NHS Employers. (2023). Pay scales for 2023/24. London: NHS Employers. www.nhsemployers.org/articles/pay-scales-202324.

Palmer, W., Rolewicz, L., Hemmings, N., Appleby, J. (2021). *Untapped? Understanding the Mental Health Clinical Support Workforce*. London: Nuffield Trust. www.nuffieldtrust.org.uk/sites/default/files/2021-08/clinical-support-workers-web.pdf.

Richards, M. (2020). *Diagnostics: Recovery and Renewal: Report of the Independent Review of Diagnostic Services for NHS England*. Redditch: NHS England. www.england.nhs.uk/wp-content/uploads/2020/11/diagnostics-recovery-and-renewal-independent-review-of-diagnostic-services-for-nhs-england-2.pdf.

Wilberforce, M., Abendstern, M., Tucker, S., Ahmed, S., Jasper, R., Challis, D. (2017). Support workers in community mental health teams for older people: roles, boundaries, supervision and training. *Journal of Advanced Nursing 73*, 1657–1666.

Chapter 8

Cambridge Dictionary. (2023). Allyship. Cambridge: Cambridge University Press & Assessment. https://dictionary.cambridge.org/dictionary/english/allyship.

Luthra, P. (2022). 7 ways to practice active allyship. Boston, MA: Harvard Business Review. https://hbr.org/2022/11/7-ways-to-practice-active-allyship.

Shaikh, A., Lamar, K., Maguire, E. (2023). The art of allyship: six ways to be an ally for women in tech. London: Deloitte. https://www2.deloitte.com/uk/en/insights/topics/value-of-diversity-and-inclusion/diversity-and-inclusion-in-tech/importance-of-allyship-women-in-tech.html.

Chapter 9

Abbajay, M. (2019). Mentoring matters: three essential elements of success. Forbes. www.forbes.com/sites/maryabbajay/2019/01/20/mentoring-matters-three-essential-element-of-success.

Arnold, J. C. (2014). *Why Forgive?* New York: Plough Publishing House.

Beheshti, N. (2019). Improve workplace culture with a strong mentoring program. Jersey City, NJ: Forbes. www.forbes.com/sites/nazbeheshti/2019/01/23/improve-workplace-culture-with-a-strong-mentoring-program/?sh=7685ded276b5.

Britannica. (2023). Harrogate. Chicago, IL: Britannica. www.britannica.com/place/North-Yorkshire.

Faragher, J. (2023). Proposed halt on EDI recruitment prompts concerns from health bodies. Sutton: Personnel Today. www.personneltoday.com/hr/edi-recruitment-nhs.

Health Education England. (2023). New resource from the reciprocal mentoring programme. Leeds: Health Education England. www.hee.nhs.uk/about/how-we-work/your-area/east-england/east-england-news/new-resource-reciprocal-mentoring-programme.

Keogh, T. (2022). *Kinder Conversations: Talk It Out, Without Falling Out*. Edinburgh: Kind Life Ltd.

Kline, N. (2009). *More Time to Think: A Way of Being in the World*. Thirsk: Fisher King Publishing.

NHS England. (2014). A guide to mentoring. Redditch: NHS England. https://cec.hscni.net/wp-content/uploads/2020/01/NHS_England_Mentoring_Guide_5bv5_FINAL5d.pdf.

NHS Leadership Academy. (2023). Coaching and mentoring. Leeds: NHS Leadership Academy. www.leadershipacademy.nhs.uk/programmes/coaching-and-mentoring.

NHS. (2023). Global learning opportunities. Leeds: Health Education England. https://global.hee.nhs.uk/supporting-individuals/global-fellowships.

Raju, S. A., Hey-Long, C., Jalal, M., Lau, M. S., et al. (2022). Does reverse mentoring work in the NHS: a feasibility study of clinicians in practice. *British Medical Journal Open 12*, 0, 1–6. www.researchgate.net/publication/365419214_Does_reverse_mentoring_work_in_the_NHS_a_feasibility_study_of_clinicians_in_practice.

Royal College of Nursing. (2023). RCN Cultural Ambassador Programme. London: Royal College of Nursing. www.rcn.org.uk/Professional-Development/Professional-services/RCN-Cultural-ambassador.

Sullivan, M. (2023). What are the types of mentoring? Cambridge, MA: HubSpot. https://blog.hubspot.com/the-hustle/types-of-mentoring.

Taylor, M., Mortimer, D., Walter, S. (2023). NHS Confederation response to Steven Barclay, Secretary of State for Health. www.nhsconfed.org/system/files/2023-10/20.10.23%20-%20NHS%20Confederation%20letter%20to%20The%20Rt%20Hon%20Steve%20Barclay%20MP.pdf.

UK Government. (2023). Positive action in the workplace: guidance for employers. London: UK Government. www.gov.uk/government/publications/positive-action-in-the-workplace-guidance-for-employers.

Young, M. (2013). *Shadow Side of Organisation Culture* (pp.1–2). Inverness: NHS Education for Scotland (NES).

Chapter 10

Baker, C., Kirk-Wade, E. (2023). *Mental Health Statistics: Prevalence, Services and Funding in England*. London: House of Commons Library. https://researchbriefings.files.parliament.uk/documents/SN06988/SN06988.pdf.

BMA. (2022). *Racism in Medicine*. London: British Medical Association. www.bma.org.uk/media/5746/bma-racism-in-medicine-survey-report-15-june-2022.pdf.

Carr, J., Clifton-Sprigg, J., James, J., Vujic, S. (2021). Did the vote for Brexit lead to a rise in hate crime? Bristol: Economics Observatory. www.economicsobservatory.com/did-the-vote-for-brexit-lead-to-a-rise-in-hate-crime.

Chidgey-Clark, J. (2023). Freedom to speak up: breaking down barriers. London: NHS Employers. https://www.nhsemployers.org/articles/freedom-speak-breaking-down-barriers.

Department of Health and Social Care. (2023). The NHS Constitution for England. London: Department of Health and Social Care. www.gov.uk/government/publications/the-nhs-constitution-for-england.

Gregory, A. (2022). NHS risks losing black and Asian doctors over 'intolerable' racism levels – report. *The Guardian*, 15 June 2022. www.theguardian.com/society/2022/jun/15/nhs-risks-losing-black-asian-doctors-racism-bma-report.

Jackson, S. (2023). Knowsley: asylum seekers attacked outside Merseyside hotel where anti-migrant protest erupted. London: Sky News. https://news.sky.com/story/knowsley-asylum-seekers-attacked-outside-merseyside-hotel-where-anti-migrant-protests-erupted-12835247.

Moberly, T. (2018). Doctors from ethnic minority backgrounds earn less than white colleagues. *British Medical Journal 363*. www.bmj.com/content/363/bmj.k5089.

NHS Digital. (2017). *Mental Health Act Statistics, Annual Figures 2016/17*. Leeds: NHS Digital. https://files.digital.nhs.uk/7C/6C9931/ment-heal-act-stat-eng-2016-17-summ-rep.pdf.

NHS England. (2020). *We Are the NHS: People Plan for 2020/2021 – Action for Us All*. Redditch: NHS England. www.england.nhs.uk/wp-content/uploads/2020/07/We-Are-The-NHS-Action-For-All-Of-Us-FINAL-March-21.pdf.

Qassem, T., Bebbington, P., Spiers, N., McManus, S., Jenkins, R., Dein, S. (2015) Prevalence of psychosis in black ethnic minorities in Britain: analysis based on three national surveys. *Social Psychiatry and Psychiatric Epidemiology 50*, 1057–1064. https://doi.org/10.1007/s00127-014-0960-7.

Siddique, H. (2021). 3.7m over-16s in Britain often or always feel lonely, ONS finds. *The Guardian*, 7 April 2021. www.theguardian.com/society/2021/apr/07/37m-over-16s-in-britain-often-or-always-feel-lonely-ons-finds.

Syal, R., Taylor, D. (2023). Supreme court rejects Rishi Sunak's plan to send asylum seekers to Rwanda. *The Guardian*, 15 November 2023. www.theguardian.com/uk-news/2023/nov/15/supreme-court-rejects-rishi-sunak-plan-to-deport-asylum-seekers-to-rwanda.

Chapter 11

Bhalla, K. (2020). Trust recognised as champions of race equality in national awards. Leicester: Leicestershire Partnership NHS Trust. www.leicspart.nhs.uk/news/trust-recognised-as-champions-of-race-equality-in-national-awards.

BMA. (2022). *Valuing Health: Why Prioritising Population Health Is Essential to Prosperity.* London: British Medical Association.

Centre for Ageing Better (2021). *The State of Ageing in Leeds.* Leeds: Leeds City Council. https://ageing-better.org.uk/resources/the-state-of-ageing-in-leeds

Charles, A. (2020). Integrated care systems explained: making sense of systems, places and neighbourhoods. London: The King's Fund. www.kingsfund.org.uk/publications/integrated-care-systems-explained?gclid=CjoKCQiApOyq BhDlARIsAGfnyMqivSCWS8600c5NZZqd0-EQHEOii7U_oMd8MuN_ ZmjlH6UAyY8mr4YaAg9oEALw_wcB.

Edwards, N., Buckingham, H. (2020). *Strategic Health Authorities and Regions: Lessons from History.* London: Nuffield Trust. www.nuffieldtrust.org.uk/research/strategic-health-authorities-and-regions-lessons-from-history.

Kinnair, D. (2020). *Tackling Health Inequalities for Black, Asian and Minority Ethnic Communities and Colleagues.* West Yorkshire and Harrogate Health and Care Partnership. www.wypartnership.co.uk/application/files/4316/0284/3010/bame-review-report-summary.pdf.

Magadi, J. P., Magadi, M. A. (2022). Ethnic inequalities in patient satisfaction in the UK. *medRxiv* 2022.06.20.22276629. https://doi.org/10.1101/2022.06.20.22276629.

NHS Confederation. (2021). What were clinical commissioning groups? London: NHS Confederation. www.nhsconfed.org/articles/what-are-clinical-commissioning-groups.

NHS England. (2022). Core20PLUS5 (adults) – an approach to reducing healthcare inequalities. Redditch: NHS England. www.england.nhs.uk/about/equality/equality-hub/national-healthcare-inequalities-improvement-programme/core20plus5.

Office for National Statistics. (2021). National life tables – life expectancy in the UK: 2018 to 2020. Newport: Office for National Statistics. www.ons.gov.uk/peoplepopulationandcommunity/birthsdeathsandmarriages/lifeexpectancies/bulletins/nationallifetablesunitedkingdom/2018to2020.

Public Health England. (2020). *Beyond the Data: Understanding the Impact of COVID-19 on BAME Communities.* London: PHE Publications. https://assets.publishing.service.gov.uk/media/5ee761fce90e070435f5a9dd/COVID_stakeholder_engagement_synthesis_beyond_the_data.pdf.

Rock, D., Grant, H. (2016). Why diverse teams are smarter. Boston, MA: Harvard Business Review. https://hbr.org/2016/11/why-diverse-teams-are-smarter.

Ross, S., Jabbal, J., Chauhan, K., Maguire, D., Randhawa, M., Dahir, S. (2020). *Workforce Race Inequalities and Inclusion in NHS Providers* (pp.1–88). London: The King's Fund. www.kingsfund.org.uk/sites/default/files/2020-07/workforce-race-inequalities-inclusion-nhs-providers-july2020.pdf.

Storey, J., Holti, R. (2013). *Towards a New Model of Leadership for the NHS*. Leeds: NHS Leadership Academy. www.leadershipacademy.nhs.uk/wp-content/uploads/2013/05/Towards-a-New-Model-of-Leadership-2013.pdf.

Umpleby, K., Roberts, C., Cooper-Moss, N., Chesterton, L., et al. (2023). *We Deserve Better: Ethnic Minorities with a Learning Disability and Barriers to Healthcare*. London: NHS Race & Health Observatory.

West Yorkshire Health and Care Partnership. (2020). Partnership launches new BAME Fellowship Programme to increase leadership diversity. Wakefield: West Yorkshire Health and Care Partnership. www.wypartnership.co.uk/news-and-blog/news/partnership-launches-new-bame-fellowship-programme-increase-leadership-diversity.

West Yorkshire Health and Care Partnership. (2021). Root out Racism. Wakefield: West Yorkshire Health and Care Partnership. www.wypartnership.co.uk/get-involved/root-out-racism/about-our-anti-racism-movement.

West Yorkshire Health and Care Partnership. (2023a). About NHS West Yorkshire Integrated Care Board. Wakefield: West Yorkshire Health and Care Partnership. www.westyorkshire.icb.nhs.uk/about-west-yorkshire-integrated-care-board.

West Yorkshire Health and Care Partnership. (2023b). West Yorkshire Integrated Care Strategy. Wakefield: West Yorkshire Health and Care Partnership. www.wypartnership.co.uk/publications/west-yorkshire-integrated-care-strategy.

West Yorkshire Health and Care Partnership. (n.d.). Improving health and tackling inequalities. Wakefield: West Yorkshire Health and Care Partnership. www.wypartnership.co.uk/publications/joint-forward-plan-2023/inequalities.

West, M., Bailey, S. (2022). What is compassionate leadership? London: The King's Fund. www.kingsfund.org.uk/publications/what-is-compassionate-leadership.

White, A., Erskine, S., Seims, A. (2019). *The State of Women's Health in Leeds*. Leeds: Leeds City Council.

Williams, E., Buck, D., Babalola, G., Maguire, D. (2022). What are health inequalities? London: The King's Fund. www.kingsfund.org.uk/publications/what-are-health-inequalities#long.

Chapter 12

Carnegie, D. (2006). *How to Win Friends and Influence People* (3rd edition). London: Vermilion.

ROOTS AND REBELLION

Personal Stories of Resisting Racism and Reclaiming Identity

Dawid Konotey-Ahulu, Debbie Iromlou, Hamzah Malik, Jen McPherson, Karis Walker-Stuart, Laura Godfrey-Isaacs, Margaret Drummond, Miriam Landor, T.P.K. Paul, Zita Holbourne, Zoe Lorimer

Order now at jkp.com

£12.99 | $18.95 | 192 pp | PB
ISBN 9781839972836 | eISBN 9781839972843

'In a society and time where change is not enough, inclusion is not enough, and diversity is not enough, we need to see, hear, and feel a transformational change. The stories presented here will contribute towards bringing about a collective resistance to social injustice and racism.'

– from the Foreword by Dr Arun Verma, Inclusion, Intersectionality and Impact Specialist, Editor of Anti-Racism in Higher Education

From the winners of the JKP Writing Prize, this anthology of stories speaks to the humanity and bravery found in resistance against racism and the various ways it can manifest. Spanning generations, cultures, and communities, these prize-winning personal essays explore what it means to reclaim identity through personal, heartfelt resistance.